Intergenerational Blind Spots:

Bridging the Gap for a Unified Tomorrow

Farzaneh Ghadirian

Farzaneh Ghadirian

Copyright © 2024 Farzaneh Ghadirian
Cover Design by Farzaneh Ghadirian and Ashley Jane
Formatted by Ashley Jane Aesthetics

All rights reserved. No part of this publication may be reproduced, distributed, or transmitted in any form by any means, including photocopying, recording, or other electronic methods without the prior written permission of the author, except in the case of brief quotations embodied in reviews and certain other noncommercial uses permitted by copyright law. For permission requests, please contact the author at FarzanehGhadirian2021@gmail.com.

INTERGENERATIONAL BLIND SPOTS/Farzaneh Ghadirian 1st Edition
ISBN: 978-0-6456495-6-7

Dedicated to my sons, Radin and Abtin, whose presence has been a constant reminder to overcome my blind spots, venture into the unknown, and embrace the path of self-discovery. I am grateful for your inspiration, urging me to be brave and committed to continuous development. May this book stand as a lasting reminder of the courage and resilience inherent in each of us.

Farzaneh Ghadirian

Dear Parent,

While I may not boast credentials as a psychologist or scientist, I share the journey of parenthood with you and hold certification as a life coach at the AACT level by the Association for Coaching (AC), a part of the Global Coaching & Mentoring Alliance (GCMA). Like you, I've faced the complexities of self-discovery, navigated my children through their challenges, and overcome personal obstacles. Throughout this experience, I've learned the importance of self-awareness, self-care, and effective communication in handling challenges and helping my children understand and navigate their own.

I've crafted this book as a journey through self-exploration, drawing from my experiences and interactions with others. Through my coaching endeavours, I've gained profound insights into intergenerational blind spots. Connecting these dots, I've created a mind map to assist others in uncovering their blind spots and navigating them with care.

In my coaching journey, I've learned that it just takes one person to recognise the patterns of their programming, to become a catalyst for change and reshape their legacy. This book is a heartfelt invitation to embark on a transformative journey, providing the tools to create a brighter future for the generations that follow.

Respectfully,

Farzaneh Ghadirian
https://www.innerharmonycoaching.com.au

Farzaneh Ghadirian

About the Book:

This book delves into the concept that parents sometimes struggle to fully grasp their children's challenges or needs, creating a blind spot in their understanding. Similarly, parents might not readily pick up on their children's emotions or the obstacles they face until it's too late. This lack of awareness can lead to a disconnect between parents and their children, leaving the latter feeling unsupported and misunderstood. Understanding our children requires recognising our own 'blind spots' and actively seeking out their perspectives and emotions. This approach strengthens the parent-child connection, ensuring that children feel acknowledged and heard.

In our daily lives, acknowledging that we may lack complete information is crucial. Being open to feedback and suggestions and remaining flexible for the sake of better outcomes is essential. Recognising our limitations and embracing different perspectives helps us navigate our blind spots, reducing potential difficulties in our daily experiences.

Furthermore, this book doesn't seek to lay blame on either us or our parents. Instead, it promotes conscious parenting and sheds light on intergenerational blind spots. Blame tends to trigger negative thinking and self-doubt, obstructing personal development and impeding positive mental restructuring. Instead of assigning blame, it's crucial to pinpoint the root causes and work on implementing solutions. This approach fosters a more conducive environment for mental restructuring and growth. The book delves into ways individuals can cultivate mindfulness and awareness in their actions and responses, nurturing healthy and positive relationships with others.

Farzaneh Ghadirian

Chapters:

1. Unravelling The Psychology of Blind Spots: Understanding Our Mental Biases
2. The Transmission of Behaviour: How Our Actions Impact Our Children's Behavioural Patterns
3. Breaking the Chains: Unravelling Repetitive Patterns for Lasting Change
4. The Influence of Childhood Environment: How Our Flaws Shape Our Children's Worldview
5. The Far-Reaching Consequences of Self-Rejection: Understanding the Impact on Our Physical, Mental, and Spiritual Well-Being
6. The Impact of Feeling Undeserved and Breaking the Victimhood Cycle
7. Overcoming Our Blind Spots: Strategies for Self-Reflection and Improvement
8. Nurturing Empathy in Children - The Cornerstone of Resilience
9. The Delicate Art of Vulnerability in Parenting: Nurturing Healthy Behaviour in Our Children While Avoiding Oversharing
10. The Power of Positive Reinforcement: Fostering Virtuous Behaviour in Our Children While Avoiding the Pitfalls of Negative Reinforcement
11. The Dangers of Shame-Based Parenting: Breaking the Cycle of Negative Behaviour
12. The Impact of Trauma: Addressing Our Own and Our Children's Past Wounds
13. The Power of Forgiveness: Healing Relationships and Promoting Positive Behaviour
14. The Role of Discipline in Shaping Behaviour: Finding a Balance Between Structure and Compassion
15. The Importance of Self-Care for Parents: Maintaining Our Own Mental Health to Better Support Our Kids
16. The Long-Term Impact of Blind Spots: Recognising the Consequences for Future Generations
17. Creating a Better Future: Nurturing Self-Awareness and Positive Behaviour in Our Children

Farzaneh Ghadirian

According to Dr. Carlfred Broderick, a transitional character is a person who, within a single generation, disrupts a destructive pattern within their family or lineage. This individual manages to overcome or "metabolise" the negative influences or trauma that may have affected previous generations, ensuring that the harmful aspects are not passed down to their children. Transitional characters break the cycle of destructive patterns, providing a foundation for future generations to lead more positive and productive lives.

The idea behind a transitional character is closely related to the concept of intergenerational trauma. The focus is on how one person's ability to navigate and overcome trauma can positively impact the trajectory of their family's history. Instead of perpetuating negative patterns, these individuals actively work to filter out the destructive elements, contributing to the creation of a more supportive and healthier family environment.

In the broader context of healing from trauma, the acknowledgment and understanding of intergenerational patterns can be crucial. Recognising the role of transitional characters and their impact on breaking destructive cycles is an important step toward fostering resilience and creating a foundation for healing within families and communities.

Farzaneh Ghadirian

Chapter 1
Unravelling the Psychology of Blind Spots: Navigating Mental Biases

A behavioural blind spot, a fascinating psychological phenomenon, unfolds when an individual is unable to acknowledge their behavioural shortcomings or deficiencies. This implicit prejudice can lead to erroneous judgments and decision-making errors, creating a ripple effect that manifests in various social and emotional challenges. Poor decision-making decreased productivity, and disrupted relationships are just a few of the consequences stemming from these blind spots. At its core, a behavioural blind spot often emerges from an individual's tendency to overestimate their capabilities while simultaneously underestimating those of others. This skewed perception fosters a heightened sense of self-importance and a lack of empathy for others' experiences. Individuals harbouring behavioural blind spots may remain oblivious to the impact of their actions on others and struggle to comprehend the emotions and perspectives of those in their immediate environment. Moreover, those grappling with behavioural blind spots often find it challenging to recognise their errors and accept responsibility for them. Instead, they may hastily point fingers at others, deflecting blame and eroding trust and respect in relationships and families.

For parents, the implications of behavioural blind spots are far-reaching, potentially hindering their children's development. These effects include impeding the ability of children to take responsibility for their actions and decisions, fostering impulsivity and risk-taking tendencies, and making it challenging for them to acknowledge and learn from mistakes. Understanding and addressing our own behavioural blind spots can empower us to be better parents and educators, paving the way for the maturation of our children into responsible and conscientious individuals. By delving into the intricacies of these psychological nuances, we embark on a journey towards fostering healthier dynamics in our families and broader social circles.

We're all familiar with the fact that adolescence is marked by rapid transformations in an individual's physical appearance, mental state, emotional well-being, and interpersonal relationships. This phase involves notable physical changes, including swift growth, alterations in body structure and size, and the onset of puberty. Simultaneously, cognitive abilities undergo enhancements in reasoning, cerebral thought, and problem-solving.

As adolescents gain more independence, their emotional development is influenced, leading to heightened experiences of happiness, sadness, frustration, and rage compared to earlier years. However, their burgeoning need for autonomy often clashes with the desire to connect with peers, creating upheaval in their social lives. This information is well-established and likely encountered through various sources, be it the media or literature. Nothing ground-breaking, right? But what unfolds when a child enters adolescence under the guidance of parents who have spent their entire lives operating from blind spots? How does our own inability to see hinder our capacity to engage meaningfully with our growing children?

When a child grows up in an environment where their parents have grappled with the effects of their blind spots, developing healthy coping strategies becomes a considerable challenge. Difficulties in emotional regulation may lead them to resort to unhealthy mechanisms such as substance abuse, avoidance of confrontations, aggressive behaviour, or even self-harm. Forming meaningful connections becomes a struggle, as does the ability to trust others. Additionally, challenges may arise in setting healthy boundaries, making decisions, and finding solutions to problems. In homes where parents are unknowingly dealing with their traumatic experiences, the long-term mental and emotional well-being of the child is at risk, making this environment detrimental to their overall development. A young person feeling responsible for their parent's mental health often takes on the role of a caregiver. They may assume responsibilities beyond their years, aiding their parents with errands, providing emotional support, and acting as a sounding board. In some cases, they might actively participate in family decision-making, offering guidance to family members and even assuming a leadership role. The impact of this can be both positive and negative. Exposure to such responsibilities can instil a strong sense of responsibility and valuable lessons, contributing positively to their future relationships. The child may experience a sense of accomplishment, and the parents may appreciate the additional support.

However, taking on more responsibilities than one can handle may lead to excessive tension and feeling overburdened. The child may experience regret if they fail to meet their parents' expectations, struggling to balance their own needs with those of their parents. This can result in a mix of regret and resentment. Unresolved feelings from this period can impede the establishment of healthy relationships in adulthood, triggering a domino effect of negative emotions and behaviours, including anxiety, melancholy, and low self-esteem. As the individual grapples with managing these emotions, it becomes challenging to trust others and form meaningful connections. Reluctance to take risks or pursue personal interests further hinders the ability to form close bonds with others.

This complex situation presents a grey area that is challenging for adults to fully comprehend. The underlying causes of life's obstacles may not be entirely clear, making it difficult to determine the right course of action for personal growth and life realignment. Reframing current struggles into empowering narratives might seem daunting, creating an experience that feels impossible to navigate.

Let's discuss how parents can transmit their traumatic experiences to their children, explore the concept of parents' blind spots, and understand the root causes of these dynamics.

Trauma, in essence, is the response that individuals exhibit when confronted with an overwhelmingly distressing situation that surpasses their coping abilities. This response can encompass physical, psychological, or emotional harm. Various events, ranging from physical or sexual assault to natural disasters, severe accidents, conflicts, or even migration, can qualify as traumatic experiences. The aftermath of a traumatic event can elicit diverse responses, spanning from physical symptoms to enduring effects on mental health.

Emotional trauma, a subset of psychological distress, arises from exposure to traumatic events, whether in the past or unfolding in the present. Trauma can result from a singular event, like a natural disaster, or chronic stress, such as abuse or neglect—both have the potential to be traumatic. Emotional trauma often accompanies feelings of dread, helplessness, sadness, guilt, and rage. Individuals with post-traumatic stress disorder (PTSD) may also grapple with intrusive thoughts, flashbacks, nightmares, and avoidance of specific people, places, or activities.

Unresolved trauma forms a construct that can limit one's potential for personal growth, essentially trapping individuals in the past. Symptoms of unresolved trauma manifest in various ways, affecting cognition, emotions, and physical well-being. Those who haven't addressed past trauma may experience physical ailments like bodily tension, headaches, or insomnia. Mentally, they may contend with challenges in concentration, decision-making, intrusive thoughts, and trust issues. On an emotional level, individuals with unresolved trauma might feel overwhelmed, irritable, anxious, and disconnected from their surroundings.

Now, considering how parents' traumatic experiences can impact their children, it becomes evident that unaddressed trauma in parents can inadvertently influence their parenting styles and behaviours. Parents operating from a place of unresolved trauma may struggle with emotional regulation, impacting their ability to provide a secure and nurturing environment for their children. These challenges can contribute to the transmission of trauma across generations, forming a complex interplay between the parents' experiences and the well-being of their children. Parent's blind spots, rooted in their own unresolved trauma, can further complicate the dynamic, influencing how they perceive and respond to their children's needs. The traumatic experiences our parents endured can deeply impact not only us but also our children, perpetuating a cycle of trauma passed from one generation to the next. When our parents struggle to regulate their emotions due to past traumas, their responses to our behaviour may become overly emotional or intense. This can adversely affect our relationships within our families, leading to feelings of apprehension, anxiety, or being overwhelmed. Consequently, we may find it challenging to regulate our own emotions and may unconsciously replicate our parents' behaviour. This perpetuates the same pattern, passing on levels of dread, anxiety, and overwhelm to our own children. Breaking this cycle of trauma or confronting our blind spots can be difficult, given its deep roots and the tendency to be transmitted across generations. The reasons are that the upbringing of a parent and their childhood experiences can contribute significantly to the blind spots they carry into adulthood. These blind spots are shaped by the values, beliefs, and expectations instilled in them by both their parents and the broader community and society in which they were raised. Common challenges for parents include struggles with rigid thinking, a lack of understanding of diverse cultures or identities, an inability to see beyond their own experiences, and a reluctance to listen to their children's perspectives.

Blind spots can have both positive and negative effects. Positive blind spots may involve unrecognised skills or abilities, such as leadership, creativity, problem-solving, or communication. Conversely, negative blind spots can manifest as harmful habits or behaviours that go unnoticed. These negative blind spots have the potential to adversely affect a person's self-esteem, emotions, and relationships, as they may be engaging in detrimental behaviours without awareness. Identifying and addressing these blind spots is crucial for personal growth, fostering positive habits, and maintaining healthy relationships.

Another multifactorial aspect contributing to the development of blind spots in our behaviours is cognitive errors. These errors, often stemming from cognitive fallacies, represent mental shortcuts or patterns of reasoning that can lead to erroneous conclusions. These biases play a role in creating blind spots as they incline us towards decision-making based on personal preferences or preconceived notions rather than objectively evaluating all the relevant facts. This can result in decisions that prioritise our likes and dislikes over the needs of others. Furthermore, the acquisition of learned behaviours can also foster blind spots in our conduct. It is commonplace for individuals to adopt behaviours from their families, peers, or the broader culture, which may limit their understanding of how their actions impact others. In such cases, individuals may be unaware of the effects of their actions on those around them or how their behaviour might be perceived as indifferent or negative.

Additionally, our environments play a pivotal role in shaping behaviours and contributing to the formation of blind spots. Growing up in an environment that either encourages or tacitly accepts certain behaviours may hinder individuals from recognising the potential consequences of those actions. For example, if raised in an environment where condescending or dismissive treatment of others is deemed acceptable, individuals may fail to comprehend how such behaviour can be harmful. In general, blind spots can develop in our behaviours due to a variety of factors; therefore, it is essential to be aware of the potential biases and learned behaviours that can contribute to their development. If we can first identify the blind spots that exist within ourselves, we can make more conscious decisions and be more mindful of how our behaviour affects those around us.

Let's delve into the significant impact of parental blind spots on the development of adolescents during this pivotal stage. These blind spots can profoundly shape the trajectory of teenagers, potentially leading to long-term consequences that reverberate into adulthood. When adolescents lack a secure and supportive relationship with their parents, the absence of necessary guidance and structure may hinder their ability to make decisions that contribute to their overall well-being. This void increases the risk of adopting detrimental behaviours like substance abuse, engaging in criminal activities, and pursuing hazardous pursuits. Without proper guidance and support, adolescents may encounter difficulties in developing essential life skills, including communication, problem-solving, financial management, and time management. The lack of parental involvement may deprive them of the vital resources and direction required to acquire these skills. Consequently, this deficiency could impede their opportunities to build self-confidence and independence while fostering values such as respect, empathy, and resilience.

The setback in foundational skills could have far-reaching consequences for adolescents, leaving them without the necessary support and guidance to make informed decisions and navigate life's complexities independently. This deficiency may increase the likelihood of engaging in risky behaviours or developing detrimental habits, with potentially severe repercussions in the future.

To foster the acquisition of skills necessary for adolescents to become independent and successful adults, parental guidance and support play a crucial role. Additionally, adolescents' behaviours, often leaning towards obsession, can be influenced by their parents' distressing experiences and a tendency for impulsivity related to their own blind spots. Compulsive behaviours among teenagers may manifest in various forms, including hoarding, spending, gambling, lying, exercise, cleaning, eating, and other repetitive actions.

Compulsive behaviours often stem from a history of traumatic experiences, leading individuals to engage in repetitive actions as a coping mechanism. These behaviours can range from ritualistic actions to avoidance of certain activities, and in extreme cases, may involve risky coping mechanisms like self-harm or substance abuse. Changing these ingrained behaviours may prove challenging without the guidance of a trained professional, emphasising the complexity of managing compulsive behaviours, which vary from person to person. Individuals exhibiting compulsive behaviours share a common goal of maintaining a preoccupation to avoid confronting repressed concerns and emotions. These activities serve as a distraction, providing a sense of safety and security, accomplishment, and enhanced self-esteem. While engaging in responsibilities can foster a sense of responsibility and capability, it's essential to recognise that compulsive behaviours may not be uniformly managed, given the unique responses to stress.

Parents who keep their children's schedules busy may be attempting to distract themselves from personal issues or fill a void created by the absence of meaningful relationships or activities. Alternatively, they might project their hopes onto their children to live vicariously through them. However, perpetually active parents can inadvertently convey the message that constant busyness is necessary, potentially affecting children's mental health and growth. Children may become overscheduled and overstimulated, missing out on crucial learning opportunities. During adolescence, the negative impact of overscheduling can be substantial. Teens may lack the chance to learn a healthy life balance and essential life lessons, hindering their ability to make wise decisions as they age. To support adolescents with low self-esteem and confidence, it is crucial to create a safe and supportive environment. This involves providing structure, setting clear expectations, and offering praise and encouragement. Strong communication between adolescents and adults allows for open discussions about emotions, challenges, and accomplishments, fostering self-esteem and confidence through engaging activities and skill development.

However, none of these positive changes can take place unless parents actively address their blind spots, enhance their knowledge and understanding of parenting, grasp the needs of their children, and display a readiness to adapt their parenting methods to evolving circumstances. By identifying and eliminating our blind spots, we not only gain a deeper understanding of our own motivations, behaviours, and the ramifications of our decisions but also recognise how our preconceived notions and biases might impact our choices and how others perceive our actions. Increasing awareness of our blind spots empowers us to make more informed decisions that account for not just our needs but also those of others. Through a heightened understanding of our biases and motivations, we can foster healthier relationships with our children.

Chapter 2
The Transmission of Behaviour: How Our Actions Impact Our Children's Behavioural Patterns

Our attachment to our blind spots can be understood as a manifestation of our need for stability and security, and our blind spots can be seen as a reflection of the beliefs and values that lay beneath the surface of our consciousness. We have a propensity to fight against change and to cling to the things that are already recognisable to us, even if doing so is not always in our best interests. We may have become so accustomed to our beliefs and ideals that we fail to recognise how they constrain our perspective. This can lead to an inability to accurately assess certain circumstances or to think creatively about alternative solutions, both of which can be detrimental to one's ability to effectively solve problems.

This may be because our blind spots provide us with a sense of security and familiarity. This can mean that we are hesitant to embrace the potential changes that can come with confronting our blind spots. This can be a problem because these changes can be beneficial. In addition, recognising and confronting our blind spots can be unsettling and difficult, and the fact that this can make us resistant to change is another potential outcome.

When we are emotionally connected to the things that cause us blind spots, we may be resistant to change even when that change is in our best interest. It's possible that we refuse to acknowledge the errors we've made, or that we're too set in our ways to attempt something different. Either we are unwilling to acknowledge the flaws in our thinking or we are too afraid to take risks because we are fearful of being criticised. It's also possible that we're unwilling to take accountability for our actions, preferring, instead, to stay within the confines of our comfort zone. In addition, we might be too attached to the achievements we've had in the past to see how the strategies we're using now might not be as successful as they once were. All of these things have the potential to prevent us from expanding our horizons and maturing, keeping us mired in the same routines and putting a cap on our potential. Furthermore, our blind spots can be a source of pride, a way to validate our identity, and a way to safeguard ourselves from the judgements of others.

How did we become so focused on our flaws? Is it due to genetics or factors in the environment?

A child's upbringing and development are profoundly shaped by the environment in which they grow up. The conditions of their upbringing can significantly influence various aspects of their development, encompassing physical and mental health, academic performance, social skills, relationships, and behaviour. Optimal development occurs when children are placed in safe environments, nurturing, and intellectually stimulating. In healthy surroundings, children have the opportunity to learn, explore, and reach their maximum potential. They thrive when given the freedom to express their individuality and creativity. A positive environment is characterised by nurturing elements that provide a sense of acceptance and stability. Such an atmosphere should also offer stimulation through a range of activities—physical, mental, and social—that challenge and engage them. Moreover, a positive environment involves acknowledging and rewarding children for their efforts and achievements. It includes providing access to resources and support systems that empower them to realise their highest potential. In essence, positive environments for children are those that foster growth, provide encouragement, and create a foundation for their overall well-being. On the flip side, children raised in unhealthy environments—marked by chaos, neglect, or abuse—often face a spectrum of physical and mental health challenges in adulthood. These adverse conditions can significantly impede a child's development, impacting both their physical well-being and mental health over the long term. Such environments may lead to issues like malnutrition, compromised general health, and weakened immune systems during childhood. Furthermore, there's an increased risk of developing mental health conditions such as anxiety, depression, and post-traumatic stress disorder. Moreover, the impact extends to cognitive development, contributing to negative educational outcomes and fostering social and emotional difficulties. In these unfavourable circumstances, children may find it challenging to establish positive relationships and learn effective coping mechanisms for stress. A child's path to a successful and healthy life can be markedly hindered when they grow up in an unhealthy environment, further influencing their overall development.

A child's development is significantly influenced by genetic factors. It is widely accepted that an individual's genetic composition can shape various traits, including personality, temperament, and physical attributes. The characteristics a person possesses, both in terms of appearance and behaviour, are directly tied to their genetic makeup and are inherited accordingly. Physical traits like eye colour, hair colour, height, and body shape are clear examples of features that can be linked to an individual's unique genetic code. Moreover, a person's personality traits and psychological attributes, such as intelligence, empathy, and creativity, are also predetermined by their genetic makeup. In the context of parenting, the specific genetic characteristics passed on to a child by one or both parents can influence the child's development. For instance, a child's inherent inclination toward certain activities, like playing a musical instrument or engaging in sports, can be attributed to their genetic predisposition. Additionally, a child's genes can contribute to their level of anxiety, emotional regulation, and susceptibility to certain disorders. Thus, genetic factors play a significant role in shaping the outcome of a child's development during the parenting process.

Our inclination to operate within our blind spots is a result of various factors, with genetics and our living environment playing pivotal roles. Each person is genetically unique, possessing distinct physical, mental, and emotional characteristics that shape how they perceive and interact with the world. These inherent differences, such as having a strong sense of intuition or being more analytical, contribute to the existence of blind spots in our perception, influencing our decisions and communication. Simultaneously, the environment in which we live, both offline and online, also contributes to the formation of blind spots. Constant exposure to diverse influences and stimuli, whether positive or negative, has the potential to shape our beliefs, attitudes, and values, creating blind spots in our worldview. For example, frequent exposure to unfavourable information may lead to increased mistrust or caution in unfamiliar situations, while positive messages and influences may foster a more accepting and trusting outlook. In essence, our genetic makeup, and the environment we inhabit collaboratively contribute to the existence of blind spots in our understanding and interaction with the world.

Another significant factor contributing to our lack of awareness and shaping our egos is the environment in which we reside. This setting plays a crucial role in influencing our perspectives, values, beliefs, and attitudes, thereby impacting our blind spots and egos. For instance, if we live in an environment that reinforces specific behaviours or attitudes, we are more likely to engage in those behaviours and adopt corresponding attitudes. This can result in an inflated ego and a distorted self-perception. Moreover, our living environment influences how we perceive our self-worth and cope with criticism and failure, shaping our sense of identity. It moulds our concepts about the world and our role in it, affecting our views on authority figures, conflict resolution, and relationships. Additionally, it influences our aspirations, goal prioritisation, and approach to realising our dreams. The individuals with whom we interact and surround ourselves also play a role in shaping our ego and blind spots. Being in the company of people with low self-esteem or a pessimistic outlook on life can impact our perspective, contributing to the development of our ego and blind spots.

The human ego is often considered the core of one's self-perception, representing a crucial aspect of personal identity. Developing the ego involves enhancing this fundamental part of the individual. It serves as a mental function that grants people a sense of their unique identity and an awareness of their value in the world. The ego is a complex element of the psyche, playing a vital role in various aspects of human behaviour, including reasoning, decision-making, and abstract thinking. Moreover, the ego serves a protective role, shielding individuals from feelings of anxiety, insecurity, and inferiority. It contributes to the development of self-esteem, self-confidence, and the preservation of a sense of autonomy and control. Beyond these functions, the ego helps us define our identity and derive meaning from our experiences. As a crucial defence mechanism, it aids in managing emotions and safeguarding against the adverse effects of stress and anxiety. Ultimately, the ego acts as a valuable resource, facilitating positive social interactions and guiding choices in our best interests.

Moreover, the ego serves as a potent psychological mechanism, aiding individuals in navigating the complexities of daily life. It acts as a mediator between the conscious and subconscious mind, allowing people to process emotions and gain an understanding of their surroundings and relationships. By distinguishing between reality and imagination, the ego enhances our ability to make rational decisions and manage our emotions effectively. Additionally, it instils a sense of safety, fostering individuals' feelings of protection and security in their environment. A strong sense of autonomy, facilitated by the ego, enables more successful interactions with others. A healthy ego exhibits self-awareness, encompassing knowledge of one's strengths, weaknesses, and beliefs, along with an accurate perception of personal boundaries. High self-esteem involves trusting our choices, embracing oneself regardless of circumstances, and deriving self-worth from achievements. Self-regulation entails expressing feelings healthily, managing stress, and controlling impulses. Self-direction involves setting and pursuing goals, making decisions, and taking responsibility for one's life. These skills are interconnected with self-confidence, a sense of inner security, self-efficacy, the belief in one's ability to accomplish tasks and the confidence to exert the effort required.

Conversely, an unbalanced ego in human manifests as an inflated sense of self-importance and entitlement, leading to a distorted worldview. Individuals with an imbalanced ego may perceive themselves as superior, prioritising their needs and goals over others. They struggle with criticism, evade accountability, and exhibit an unhealthy obsession with success and recognition. Characteristics of an imbalanced ego include grandiosity, entitlement, difficulty accepting responsibility, an excessive focus on success, lack of empathy, and self-centeredness. These traits can result in difficulties forming meaningful relationships, a lack of self-awareness, risky behaviours, emotional instability, low self-esteem, challenges in handling stress, distorted reality perception, and hindered personal growth and development.

In certain situations, children may adopt unhealthy egoic behaviours from their parents, especially if raised in an environment where one or both parents exhibit imbalanced and egoistic behaviour. For example, a child might observe their parents displaying problematic behaviours such as narcissism, perfectionism, or entitlement. How parents respond to challenging situations can also serve as a model for the child's own reactions and coping mechanisms. Additionally, children may internalise the beliefs and values of their parents, including detrimental egocentric ones. Another possibility is that parents might directly teach their children problematic egocentric behaviours, such as using criticism or sarcasm. Furthermore, the unhealthy egoic actions of a child's parents can inflict emotional and psychological harm, affecting the child. This may manifest as feelings of inadequacy, insecurity, or shame directly linked to the parent's behaviour. As a result of these experiences, the child may develop a mistrust in their own capabilities and struggle to form meaningful relationships. In the long term, this could lead the child to develop an unhealthy egoic identity, potentially resulting in increased emotional and psychological distress. This distress might manifest in behaviours such as avoiding difficult situations or engaging in self-destructive actions as a coping mechanism. When a child employs avoidance, numbness, or other self-destructive behaviours as coping mechanisms, it can lead to disengagement from activities they once enjoyed, avoidance of places or people they were once comfortable with and increased social isolation. Additionally, they may numb themselves to challenging emotions like sadness or fear, potentially leading to more severe mental health issues such as depression, anxiety, and post-traumatic stress disorder (PTSD) over time.

These coping mechanisms can also manifest in physical problems like fatigue, headaches, and sleep disturbances. The long-term consequence of relying on such coping mechanisms is the inability to process and recover from traumatic experiences, resulting in the accumulation of unresolved pain that contributes to further emotional challenges.

Self-destructive behaviours encompass actions that can negatively impact an individual's life and well-being. While commonly associated with substance abuse or physical harm like cutting, there are subtler yet equally harmful examples. Obsessive cleaning, perfectionism, and the relentless pursuit of wealth and status through education and employment fall under this category. Excessive cleanliness, ranging from constant organising to compulsive disinfecting, may seem harmless but can become an obsession, consuming significant time and energy at the expense of meaningful relationships and other productive activities. Perfectionism involves the relentless pursuit of an unattainable level of perfection, leading to frustration and dissatisfaction, often hindering the completion of projects. The pursuit of wealth and status, while seemingly positive, can turn self-destructive as it may lead to an unhealthy obsession with money and titles, sacrificing relationships and overall life quality.

Less obvious self-destructive behaviours, often practised unconsciously, can lead to negative consequences and may be challenging to recognise as self-destructive. While these actions may not be immediately apparent, they can become routine and may initially seem advantageous but eventually cause harm. Examples include procrastination, avoidance, people-pleasing, perfectionism, and overworking. These behaviours may be difficult to identify as self-destructive because they can be mistaken for positive traits, such as striving for excellence or being hardworking. However, when practised excessively, they can contribute to physical, mental, and emotional exhaustion, leading to burnout, anxiety, and depression. Additionally, individuals may deny these self-destructive behaviours due to a fear of judgment and a desire to maintain a positive self-image.

Children who are brought up by parents who are not aware of their own feelings or who live in environments that are out of balance may exhibit a variety of emotions and behaviours. They frequently experience feelings of disorientation and disorientation, as well as a lack of a sense of identity and protection. They may also struggle to trust their own feelings and thoughts, instead depending on the reactions of their parents or the environment around them to understand how to behave or how to feel. This can contribute to feelings of depression, anxiety, and a lack of self-worth. They may also exhibit behaviours such as withdrawal, avoidance, aggression, and acting out. It is essential for them to learn how to establish a connection with their deeper selves so that they can cultivate a sense of self-awareness, recognise who they are, and comprehend the requirements of their situation.

Children raised in unbalanced or unhealthy environments may require the support of a trained professional to develop resilience and cultivate self-trust. While this can pose challenges, it is crucial to offer the necessary assistance to these children. Such children are more likely to engage in self-subscription and seek external sources of enjoyment to fill the void within them. Growing up in such environments, these youngsters often express a sense of disconnection from their own identity. This disconnection can stem from various factors, including a lack of secure attachment with their parents, difficulty processing their own feelings and thoughts, or an environment lacking healthy boundaries and structure. In these circumstances, children may lack the space or opportunity to establish a strong sense of self. Consequently, they frequently turn to external sources for comfort, pleasure, and a sense of identity. This reliance can lead to negative feelings and behaviours like withdrawal, aggression, and acting out. While practicing self-abandonment and seeking external pleasure may temporarily fill the void caused by their unbalanced environment, it doesn't provide a lasting solution.

A child's development can be hindered by a negative environment, limiting their ability to learn, explore, and reach their full potential. Conversely, a positive environment can enhance a child's development. Genetic factors also play a crucial role, in influencing physical and behavioural traits, as well as personality and psychological characteristics. In terms of the ego, a balanced one exhibits self-awareness, self-esteem, self-regulation, self-direction, self-confidence, and self-efficacy. Conversely, an unbalanced ego involves an exaggerated sense of self-importance and entitlement, distorting one's perception of reality. Children may inherit unhealthy egoic behaviours from parents with unbalanced, egoistic tendencies. This can lead to feelings of inadequacy, insecurity, shame, and mistrust in the child's abilities, making it challenging to form meaningful relationships. Children may also adopt unhealthy egoic coping strategies, such as avoidance and numbing, with long-term negative effects on their physical and mental health. Recognizing the impact of both environmental and genetic factors on the ego is crucial. Providing children with a secure and nurturing environment is essential for their growth. By exploring our blind spots in a supportive atmosphere, we can broaden our perspectives, embrace new ideas, and create a more fulfilling life for ourselves and those around us.

In essence, recognising intergenerational influences on behaviour and personality dynamics involves closely observing our own actions and those of our surroundings. Identifying patterns and similarities in responses to various circumstances, as well as exploring how these responses evolve over time, provides valuable insights. Additionally, examining the correlations between our genetic background and behaviour, such as the impact of genetic disorders, helps uncover the complex interplay between genetics and environment. Our blind spots emerge from this intricate interplay of genetic factors and living conditions. While we may not alter our genetic makeup, we possess the capacity to actively shape our environment for better health and well-being. Understanding these blind spots enables us to pinpoint developmental areas, fostering a more positive and productive mindset. Moreover, viewing blind spots as opportunities for growth and learning is essential. Acknowledging them allows us to delve into our beliefs and biases and understand their influence on decisions and actions. Becoming aware of how blind spots affect relationships with others empowers us to bridge potential divides and foster greater understanding.

Farzaneh Ghadirian

Chapter 3
Breaking the Chains:
Unravelling Repetitive Patterns for Lasting Change and Their Impact on Our Children

This chapter embarks on a journey to explore the intricacies of repetitive patterns, unveiling their influence on our lives and, more significantly, on the lives of our children. We will delve into the psychological underpinnings of these patterns, seeking avenues for breaking free and instigating transformative change.

Repetitive patterns can become a go-to way for individuals to deal with trauma, acting as a method of self-comfort and a means to regain a sense of control. When people lack the necessary skills to address their trauma effectively, these patterns tend to become automatic responses, offering a brief escape from overwhelming emotions.

The impact of trauma on the brain is substantial, influencing perceptions in several ways:

Trauma can cause the amygdala, a brain region linked to emotions, to become hypersensitive. This heightened sensitivity leads to stronger emotional reactions and an intensified "fight or flight" response. The functioning of the hippocampus, crucial for memory and contextualising experiences, is affected by trauma. This interference can result in the re-living of traumatic events or difficulties in creating coherent narratives about them.
The prefrontal cortex, responsible for decision-making, impulse control, and emotional regulation, may suffer impairments due to

trauma. This can result in challenges in managing emotions and making rational judgments.

Changes in neurotransmitter levels, triggered by trauma, impact mood regulation. This alteration may contribute to conditions like anxiety, depression, or other mental health challenges. Trauma can instil a heightened perception of threat in various situations, even when immediate danger is absent. This constant alertness influences how individuals interpret and respond to their surroundings.

Repetitive patterns often serve as maladaptive coping mechanisms, initially developed as survival strategies. While these patterns might offer momentary relief, they can impede long-term healing by perpetuating unhealthy cycles.

Understanding Repetitive Patterns

The exploration of repetitive patterns opens a gateway to understanding the intricate workings of human behaviour and cognition. At its core, repetitive patterns are engrained sequences in both our actions and thoughts, silently influencing the trajectory of our lives.

Repetitive patterns in behaviour emerge from a complex interplay of environmental factors, learned responses, and cognitive processes. Examining these patterns through a behavioural lens reveals them as learned behaviours intricately woven into the fabric of our daily lives, each thread reinforced by past experiences. From the behavioural perspective, repetition serves a fundamental purpose—it establishes a sense of familiarity and predictability, fashioning a psychological comfort zone. This comfort zone becomes a refuge, a space where actions become automatic, and responses feel familiar. Unpacking the behavioural aspect entails a deep dive into the intricate mechanisms of reinforcement. Behaviours are reinforced through a delicate dance of positive and negative reinforcements, each playing a role in cementing the repetition of certain actions.

Positive reinforcement involves the receipt of rewards or favourable outcomes, encouraging the recurrence of specific behaviours. This could range from the pleasure derived from a particular activity to the positive reactions received from others. In essence, the joy or benefit associated with a behaviour becomes a motivating force for repetition. Conversely, negative reinforcement involves the removal of aversive stimuli or the avoidance of undesirable outcomes, reinforcing the repetition of certain behaviours. The relief or escape from discomfort becomes a powerful motivator, compelling individuals to engage in actions that alleviate stress or unpleasant experiences.

The psychological comfort derived from repetitive patterns is, in part, a product of these reinforcement mechanisms. Actions associated with positive outcomes, or the avoidance of negative consequences become deeply ingrained. The behavioural foundation of repetitive patterns, therefore, lies in the intricate dance of reinforcement, shaping our actions and responses in the theatre of our daily lives.

Delving into the cognitive underpinnings of repetitive patterns unveils a profound connection with cognitive schemas and biases. At the core of this intricate interplay are cognitive schemas—mental frameworks that serve as lenses through which individuals interpret information. These schemas, once established, intertwine with repetitive patterns, creating a reciprocal relationship where each influences and shapes the other.

Repetitive patterns, once woven into the fabric of our behaviour, mould and are moulded by these cognitive frameworks. As individuals navigate their experiences, these frameworks act as interpretative guides, influencing how events are perceived and understood. The cognitive schema becomes a template that reinforces the recurrence of specific behaviours and responses. The cognitive interplay extends further into the realm of cognitive biases—innate predispositions to think in particular ways. Repetitive patterns, firmly anchored in cognitive schemas, align with these biases, creating a reinforcing loop that solidifies the persistence of specific thought patterns. Individuals develop a cognitive comfort with familiar ways of thinking, often defaulting to these established patterns as a cognitive shortcut.

Understanding how repetitive patterns become entrenched in cognitive processes involves recognising the reciprocal relationship between cognitive schemas and the repetition of behaviours. These cognitive frameworks act as architects, constructing the mental landscape through which individuals navigate, interpret, and respond to the world around them. As cognitive biases reinforce these patterns, the intricate dance between cognition and repetition continues, shaping the contours of our thought processes in enduring ways.

Unravelling the psychodynamic dimensions of repetitive patterns delves into the realm of unconscious processes, drawing insights from Sigmund Freud's concept of repetition compulsion. At its core, the psychodynamic perspective posits that repetitive patterns can be understood as manifestations of unconscious inclinations, revealing hidden layers of unresolved conflicts and psychological intricacies.

Freud's notion of repetition compulsion unveils a compelling aspect of these patterns—an unconscious drive to re-enact unresolved conflicts from the past. From a psychodynamic lens, these repetitions are not mere coincidences, but rather symbolic representations deeply rooted in the unconscious. Exploring these patterns entails deciphering the symbolic language embedded within recurrent behaviours, providing a gateway to the uncharted territories of the psyche. Psychodynamic theories propose that repetitive patterns may serve as symbolic expressions of unresolved psychological issues. By closely examining the recurrent themes in behaviour or the recurring motifs in dreams, one can unveil the symbolic messages concealed within these patterns. Each repetition becomes a clue, offering glimpses into the hidden recesses of the psyche and the lingering echoes of past experiences.

Exploring the neurological implications of repetitive patterns unveils a fascinating landscape where the brain's remarkable plasticity and adaptability play a pivotal role in both the formation and persistence of these recurring behaviours and thoughts. The neurological dimension provides valuable insights into the intricate mechanisms that underlie the establishment and resilience of repetitive patterns. At the core of this neurological phenomenon is the concept of neuroplasticity—the brain's ability to reorganise itself and form new neural connections in response to experience. Repetition acts as a catalyst for neuroplastic changes by reinforcing specific neural pathways. As actions or thoughts are repeated over time, these pathways undergo structural modifications, resulting in increased synaptic efficiency and strengthened connections. This process creates a neurobiological efficiency in processing, making the repeated patterns more automatic and resistant to change. Understanding the neural mechanisms involved sheds light on why patterns become deeply ingrained and challenging to alter. The strengthened neural pathways represent a form of cognitive economy, where the brain prioritises efficiency by relying on familiar routes. Consequently, breaking free from entrenched patterns requires interventions that address the underlying neural architecture.

Neuroscientific research provides valuable insights into the malleability of these patterns and suggests potential interventions to rewire entrenched neural pathways. Techniques such as cognitive restructuring, mindfulness, and targeted therapeutic interventions leverage neuroplasticity to introduce new patterns and disrupt the automaticity of established ones. By consciously engaging in activities that promote new neural connections, individuals can gradually reshape their cognitive landscape and create pathways that align with desired behavioural changes.

Transmission to the Next Generation

Understanding the transmission of repetitive patterns to the next generation unveils a profound exploration into how behaviours, learned responses and emotional dynamics traverse family lines, creating an intergenerational cycle. This phenomenon, known as transgenerational transmission, sheds light on how children unconsciously adopt and perpetuate patterns observed in their parents, influencing their psychological and emotional development.

A child's observation of repetition compulsion patterns in their parents can significantly impact various facets of their psychological and emotional well-being. The intricate interplay between parent and child sets the stage for a complex dance of learned behaviours, shaping the child's worldview and approach to relationships. Children are remarkably impressionable, often mirroring their behaviour based on what they observe in their parents. If parents engage in repetitive and potentially unhealthy patterns, these behaviours become ingrained in the child's repertoire. The child learns and internalises these patterns, unwittingly perpetuating the cycle of repetition. The dynamics witnessed in parental relationships become a template for the child's expectations and beliefs about relationships. Repetition compulsion in parental bonds influences the child's unconscious preferences, guiding them to seek out or recreate similar relationship dynamics in their own adult life.

Exposure to repetitive negative patterns can cast a long shadow on a child's emotional well-being. The child, perceiving these patterns as sources of conflict or instability, may grapple with feelings of insecurity, anxiety, or stress. The emotional landscape shaped by these observed patterns becomes a significant aspect of the child's internal world. A child raised in an environment where parents struggle with unresolved conflicts or unhealthy coping mechanisms may lack effective models for conflict resolution. Observing the challenges faced by parents can influence the child's ability to navigate conflicts in their own life, potentially perpetuating the cycle of ineffective conflict management.

Repetitive negative patterns witnessed in parental struggles can significantly impact a child's self-esteem. The child, internalising these struggles, may develop feelings of inadequacy or a belief that similar patterns are an inevitable part of their own life. The struggle becomes intertwined with the child's perception of self-worth.

Creating New Family Narratives

As we reach the culmination of this journey, we delve into the transformative concept of crafting new family narratives. The exploration of this theme is not just a theoretical exercise but a poignant journey into the realms of real-life successes, illustrating the power of conscious effort in challenging and reframing deeply ingrained behaviours.

Within the fabric of family narratives lies the potential for profound change. Families, by collectively and consciously addressing repetitive patterns, hold the key to unlocking a future unburdened by the heavy chains of repetition.

The narrative of breaking free is one of empathy and understanding, acknowledging the struggles inherent in reshaping deeply ingrained patterns. It's a journey that extends beyond personal triumphs, encompassing the collective strength of families weaving new stories of growth and transformation. The call to action is not just an invitation but a compassionate recognition of the challenges faced by each member of the family unit.

Breaking Free: Strategies for Lasting Change

Unlocking lasting change from repetitive patterns requires a multifaceted approach, drawing on practical strategies rooted in mindfulness practices and cognitive-behavioural approaches. These strategies serve as transformative tools, not only for individuals seeking change but also for shaping a healthier trajectory in the lives of their children.

Mindfulness practices stand out as a cornerstone in breaking free from repetitive patterns. By cultivating a heightened awareness of the present moment, individuals can disrupt automatic responses rooted in these patterns. Mindfulness enables a deliberate pause, providing the mental space to choose responses consciously rather than succumbing to ingrained reactions. It serves as a powerful ally in initiating change by fostering a connection between thought and action.

Complementing mindfulness, cognitive-behavioural approaches offer a structured framework for dismantling repetitive patterns. These approaches delve into the interplay between thoughts, feelings, and behaviours, empowering individuals to identify and challenge maladaptive patterns at their roots. Through cognitive restructuring, individuals can reframe distorted thought patterns, disrupting the cycle of automatic and unhelpful responses. Neurologically, these strategies contribute to reshaping entrenched neural pathways. Mindfulness, with its focus on attention and awareness, induces neuroplasticity, the brain's capacity to adapt and reorganise. Similarly, cognitive-behavioural interventions stimulate changes in neural connections, creating more adaptive pathways. Understanding these neurological dimensions underscores the efficacy of these strategies in fostering genuine transformation.

In the realm of trauma recovery, therapy emerges as a linchpin in the process of breaking free from repetitive patterns. Trauma-focused therapy, with its targeted approach, helps individuals confront and process traumatic experiences. By delving into the emotional and cognitive aspects of trauma, this therapeutic modality guides individuals in building healthier coping mechanisms and reshaping their narratives.

Mindfulness practices within the therapeutic context further enhance emotional regulation and healing. Techniques such as mindful breathing and body scans enable individuals to anchor themselves in the present, mitigating the emotional intensity associated with traumatic memories. The integration of mindfulness into trauma-focused therapy amplifies its effectiveness in fostering resilience and empowering individuals to navigate the complexities of their journey.

Dismantling maladaptive patterns becomes a central focus within the therapeutic space. Through a nuanced exploration of experiences, individuals gain insight into the origins of these patterns, unravelling the intricate web of their emotional and behavioural responses. This process fosters a deeper understanding of oneself and lays the foundation for intentional, adaptive choices.

Empowerment lies at the heart of trauma recovery. The journey involves not only rewriting narratives but also reclaiming agency over one's life. By combining mindfulness practices, cognitive-behavioural approaches, and trauma-focused therapy, individuals embark on a comprehensive path toward lasting change. This journey, marked by self-discovery and resilience, extends beyond the individual, influencing the lives of their children by breaking the chains of intergenerational repetition. In essence, these practical strategies serve as beacons of transformation, guiding individuals toward a future defined by adaptive responses and the freedom to shape their own narratives.

Farzaneh Ghadirian

Chapter 4
The Influence of Childhood Environment: How Our Flaws Shape Our Children's Worldview

A person's mood, thinking, and behaviour can be significantly influenced by various conditions encompassed by the term "mental illness." This term encompasses a spectrum of conditions, ranging from mild to severe, that can impede a person's ability to function normally in day-to-day life activities. The development of mental illness has been associated with factors such as genetic predisposition, alterations in brain chemistry, stressful life events, traumatic experiences, and a family history of mental illness.

Our mental health is shaped not only by biological factors like genes, hormones, and brain chemistry but also by psychological elements such as stress, traumatic experiences, and personality. Additionally, social factors play a crucial role, including the dynamics of our families, relationships with peers, and the cultural context in which we live.

Biological factors that increase the likelihood of developing a mental health condition can amplify the symptoms of mental illness in an individual. For example, genes can influence whether an individual is predisposed to specific mental health conditions. Hormonal imbalances represent another aspect that might contribute to mental health issues. Changes in neurotransmitter levels have been associated with alterations in brain chemistry, which, are connected to a diverse array of mental health problems.

Mental illness shapes our blind spots, and our inability to recognise and comprehend the warning signs of mental illness is a trait that will be passed down from generation to generation. Many individuals who are struggling with mental illnesses do not even have the slightest idea that they have a problem. If it is not recognised and treated, mental illness can be passed down from parent to child and will have a significant effect on future generations. It is possible for parents to unknowingly pass on their untreated mental illness to their children through a variety of channels, such as providing insufficient care, modelling inappropriate behaviour, and passing on genetic predispositions. The transmission of mental illness from one generation to the next can have long-term repercussions. Children whose parents suffer from mental illness are more likely to have low self-esteem, anxiety, depression, and difficulty interacting socially. They might also have a difficult time making friends and succeeding academically. These kids may have a higher risk of developing mental illness as adults. Because of this, failing to understand mental illness and the mechanisms by which it is passed down from one generation to the next can have severe repercussions.

The transmission of mental disorders from one generation to the next encompasses several mechanisms, with genetic inheritance, environmental factors, and epigenetics playing pivotal roles.

The prevailing belief suggests that mental illnesses can be inherited through families due to genetic factors passed down from one generation to another. The development of mental illnesses is a complex interplay of various elements, including both genetic predisposition and environmental influences. Extensive research has identified associations between specific genes and a diverse range of mental disorders, shedding light on the intricate genetic landscape of mental health. Beyond genetics, individuals who have undergone traumatic experiences or faced high levels of stress exhibit an elevated risk of developing mental illnesses later in life. For instance, children who witness or endure violence or abuse during their formative years face an increased susceptibility to mental health issues in adulthood. The impact of environmental factors, especially adverse experiences, is substantial in shaping the mental health trajectories of individuals across generations.

In recent years, the significance of epigenetics in mental health has garnered increasing attention. This specialised field within biology delves into understanding how environmental factors can shape gene expression without altering the fundamental genetic code. This implies that specific environmental influences have the potential to be inherited across generations, potentially impacting the mental health of individuals. Epigenetics operates as a bridge between the environment and genetics, shedding light on the intricate ways in which external factors can leave a lasting imprint on gene activity. The dynamic interplay between environmental conditions and the regulation of gene expression offers a nuanced understanding of how certain influences may transcend generations, influencing the mental health outcomes of individuals over time. This evolving understanding of epigenetics underscores the interconnectedness of nature and nurture in shaping mental health. It prompts exploration into how experiences and exposures across generations can leave lasting marks on the molecular level, influencing the susceptibility to mental health conditions. As the field continues to advance, the implications of epigenetics on mental health open new avenues for research, intervention, and a more comprehensive understanding of the factors contributing to mental well-being.

Understanding the interplay of these factors provides a comprehensive view of mental health dynamics, acknowledging the bidirectional relationship between genes and environment. Psychological theories, such as the diathesis-stress model, emphasise the interaction between genetic vulnerabilities and stressful life events in precipitating mental health disorders. Additionally, the bio-psycho-social model underscores the importance of considering biological, psychological, and social factors in understanding mental health.

This integrated approach opens avenues for targeted interventions and support. Psychosocial interventions, cognitive-behavioural therapy, and resilience-building programs are examples of psychological strategies that consider both genetic predispositions and environmental influences. Moreover, understanding epigenetic mechanisms provides insights into potential therapeutic targets that bridge the biological and psychological dimensions of mental health.

We are just starting to get a better understanding of how our environments can have an impact on our mental health, but it is clear that they do. The findings of several studies suggest that children who are brought up in environments that are nurturing and supportive may develop a sense of security that assists them in coping with the challenges that are a part of everyday life. They could have better mental health as a direct result of the environment in which they live. On the other hand, being subjected to an environment that is disorganised, unstructured, and unsupportive can result in feelings of insecurity and helplessness, both of which can increase the likelihood of developing mental health issues.

Throughout the past few years, the connection between factors in one's environment and mental health has emerged as a more prominent theme. There are numerous facets of our health, such as our mental health, that are susceptible to the effects of our environment, and these facets can be observed to affect us. This is because environmental factors can affect gene expression, which in turn can affect our mental health.

Gene expression is the process by which genes are activated (turned on) or inactivated (turned off), and it occurs in every cell. It takes place when the information that is stored in our genes is transferred to proteins. Proteins are what determine the characteristics of a cell as well as the characteristics of an organism. To phrase it another way, the environment in which we live can have an effect on which genes are expressed, and the genes in question can then affect our mental health.

For instance, research has demonstrated that prolonged exposure to stress can cause changes in gene expression in the brain, which can ultimately result in the onset of depressive symptoms. There is a region of the brain called the hippocampus that is associated with memory, learning, and feelings. The expression of genes in this part of the brain can be changed by traumatic experiences as well. A recent study found that people who had traumatic experiences as children had changes in gene expression in the hippocampus. These changes in gene expression in the hippocampus may explain why these people are more likely to have mental health issues. Recent studies suggest that epigenetics may be involved in both how our brains react to stress and how we remember things. This function might also encompass how we acquire new knowledge. It has been shown that chronic stress can cause long-term changes in the brain, which can lead to a variety of issues relating to mental health such as anxiety, depression, and others.

It has been hypothesised that shifts in epigenetics are to blame for changes in brain activity, and this is consistent with the hypothesis. For instance, it has been demonstrated that prolonged exposure to stress can cause an increase in the production of particular hormones, such as cortisol, which in turn can cause changes in the expression of genes. The way in which the brain responds to stress and how we remember things can be altered as a result of these changes.

Changes in the functioning of neurotransmitters that regulate mood and behaviour, such as dopamine and serotonin, have also been linked to chronic stress. These neurotransmitters include dopamine and serotonin. Because of these changes, the individual may exhibit more aggressive behaviour and also be at a greater risk of becoming addicted. The way we react to things that happen to us and the way we perceive the world around us can both be influenced by stress. It has the potential to lead to skewed thinking as well as an inability to make rational choices. A person's ability to deal with stressful situations can also be negatively impacted, and the likelihood of developing physical health issues can rise as a result.

Both the development of our behavioural tendencies and our cognitive capacities are influenced by the environment we live in. It has the capability of either encouraging and fostering creativity or restricting our cognitive abilities and stunting our intellectual development. We are the product of our environment and the way we think and the way our brains are structured are both shaped and moulded by our environment. We are the product of the conditions in which we were raised.

Our neurobiology is influenced directly by the external environment in which we find ourselves. Changes in temperature, light, and sound, in addition to the chemicals that are present in the air that we breathe, can all affect our sensitivity. All of these factors have the potential to have an effect on the neurobiology of our bodies as well as the functioning of our brains.

The social environment that surrounds you is also an important factor. Because we are social creatures, the only way for us to learn new things and advance our knowledge is by interacting with other individuals. The simple act of interacting with other people not only prompts our bodies to produce more hormones and neurotransmitters, but it also has the potential to affect how we think and behave.

A significant influence on our neurobiology can also be exerted by the environment in which we receive our education and perform our work. New brain cells and neural pathways can be created when students are exposed to an intellectually challenging classroom setting. On the other hand, if the environment in which we learn is not stimulating, we might experience a decrease in the growth of new brain cells as well as a decline in our cognitive abilities. This could happen if the environment in which we learn is not stimulating.

The idea that we are the result of the circumstances in which we were raised has a long and illustrious history that dates back hundreds of years. To boil it down to its essential meaning, it suggests that the people and circumstances to which we are exposed in the course of our daily lives have an effect on the actions, thoughts, and beliefs that we have. This has the potential to have both positive and negative repercussions. This concept is predicated on the premise that the people and settings in which we engage, in addition to the activities and occurrences that take place within those settings, have a significant impact on who we are as individuals.

Our immediate environment consists not only of our family and friends but also of our community and society as a whole. It also encompasses the actual space that we occupy, such as our home and the community in which we live, in addition to the digital environment that we construct and with which we engage. The development of our identities is influenced in some way by each of these components in their own unique way. For instance, our family has the power to mould our values and beliefs regarding particular topics, while our community has the power to mould our beliefs regarding what is considered "normal" and "acceptable." Because our interactions with other people and our perceptions of the world around us can be influenced by our physical surroundings, our physical surroundings can also influence the development of our behaviour.

It is essential to have an understanding that the environment is always changing, and these changes frequently take on unexpected forms. This is because environmental changes frequently take place in unexpected ways. For instance, developments in technology have the potential to radically transform our surroundings and the ways in which we engage with those surroundings. Alterations in the social environment in which we find ourselves can also have an effect on the beliefs and behaviours that we engage in. For instance, the events that take place in our community or society may serve as a catalyst for us to adjust either our beliefs or our behaviour in order to be in accordance with the newly established standards.

It shouldn't come as a surprise that the environment we grow up in has a significant bearing on who we become. We are the product of our environments, and the people and things that are a part of our lives are continually shaping and moulding us into new forms. Our environment not only gives us the resources, opportunities, and motivation we need to accomplish what we set out to do, but it also has the power to either restrict or broaden those options. Our environment has a significant influence on our beliefs, values, and behaviours, and it also has the potential to have a profound effect on our personality and sense of who we are. It is essential that we acknowledge the influence that our environment has on our development because it is a significant component of who we are.

The effects of a child's upbringing in a dysfunctional household, in which the adults do not acknowledge their own mental health blind spots, can have severe and long-lasting repercussions for the child. In the field of mental health, the term "blind spot" refers to a lack of awareness or comprehension regarding one's own thoughts, feelings, and behaviours as well as those of other people. Without awareness of these blind spots in mental health, it may be extremely challenging, if not impossible, for a child to develop healthy friendships, a positive sense of who they are, and the ability to solve problems. One of the many negative effects of toxic environments on the development of a child is a noticeable decline in the child's resilience when confronted with pressure and difficulty. This is just one of the many negative effects. If a child does not have access to positive role models from which they can learn and a safe environment in which they can express their feelings, then that child's likelihood of developing anxiety, depression, and other mental health problems later in life is increased. For instance, if a child's parents do not model behaviours such as taking risks or expressing themselves emotionally, the child may be less likely to do these things on their own. If blind spots in mental health are not recognised, it may have long-term consequences for a child's social and emotional development. These consequences may last for a long time. If a child does not learn how to control their emotions and interact with others in a healthy way, it may be difficult for them to form relationships with other people that they can rely on, boost their self-confidence, and handle the stress that comes with their lives. It's possible that the end result of this will be a lack of self-esteem as well as difficulty navigating social situations. A child is more likely to experience problems with their physical health if they are raised in an unhealthy environment, in addition to the psychological effects that are caused by the environment. If a child does not have access to healthy coping mechanisms, they are more likely to engage in risky behaviours such as abusing substances, engaging in binge eating, and leading sedentary lifestyles. As a consequence of this, one's likelihood of developing obesity, diabetes, cardiovascular disease, and various other problems related to physical health may go up.

When parents aren't aware of their own mental health blind spots, it can have a significant impact on their child's development from a psychological and emotional standpoint as well as on the social interactions they have with other people. Blind spots are areas of mental illness or mental health problems that a person is either unaware of or hesitant to acknowledge because they are worried about their own mental health. The term "blind spots" refers to these areas of mental illness or mental health problems. When parents are unaware of the blind spots in their own mental health, it's possible for their children to experience feelings of instability and unease.

Children learn how to regulate their feelings and communicate with other people at a young age, and the most effective way for them to do this is to observe and imitate the behaviour of their parents. When parents are unaware of their mental health blind spots, they may engage in unhealthy behaviours such as being overly critical, having trouble controlling their emotions, or displaying signs of depression or anxiety. These behaviours can be detrimental to their children. These actions may put their children in danger in some way. Because of the anxiety and nervousness that these behaviours can instil in the child, the child may try to act in the same way as the parent in an effort to feel more secure or fit in. This is because these behaviours can instil these feelings in the child. As a consequence of this, the child may get the impression that their parent isn't there to support them, which may lead to feelings of isolation and abandonment on their part. If the parent does not act as a positive role model, it will be challenging for the child to develop positive relationships with the people who are in their immediate environment. Not to mention the fact that parents who are unaware of the blind spots in their own mental health may not be able to provide the resources and support that are necessary for their children to develop healthy mental routines as they grow up. If the child does not receive the appropriate support, it is possible that they will struggle in the future to keep their feelings in check and make choices that are in their own best interests.

Farzaneh Ghadirian

Chapter 5
The Far-Reaching Consequences of Self-Rejection:
Understanding the Impact on Our Physical, Mental, and Spiritual Well-Being

A traumatic event, by its very nature, disrupts the delicate balance of our emotional well-being. It's an experience that can range from deeply distressing to utterly shocking, and its consequences are profound. The effects of trauma can ripple through an individual's life, often triggering a wide spectrum of emotions and responses. These responses, which range from fear and anxiety to self-rejection, can be powerful and long-lasting. To truly understand the intricacies of trauma and self-rejection, we must explore how they interconnect and influence an individual's life.

Trauma, whether stemming from a specific incident or a prolonged experience, is defined by its capacity to induce extreme emotional distress, shatter our sense of security, and disrupt our daily lives. However, the emotional aftermath of trauma is not one-size-fits-all; it's a complex interplay between the individual's unique characteristics, the nature of the traumatic experience, and the time that has passed since the event.

Fear is one of the most common emotional responses to traumatic events. In the wake of trauma, individuals often find themselves grappling with an overwhelming sense of fear. This fear can be paralysing, making it difficult for individuals to regain control over their surroundings and emotional responses. It's an anxiety that can lead to social withdrawal and avoidance of situations, places, or people that might trigger distressing memories associated with the traumatic event.

Anxiety is another emotional response that frequently accompanies trauma. The pressures of daily life can leave individuals feeling overwhelmed, especially if they are already dealing with a heavy load. This constant state of anxiety leads individuals to live with an ever-present sense of impending doom as if something terrible is perpetually lurking around the corner. Remarkably, even after apparent recovery, those who've experienced traumatic events might continue to battle anxiety and panic.

Shock can be the initial response to trauma, but it can also be an enduring effect. Some individuals find it challenging to process what happened, leading to feelings of detachment and numbness. The world around them becomes distant, and they struggle to feel fully present in their own lives.

Confusion often follows in the wake of traumatic experiences, as individuals grapple with their ability to comprehend what occurred. This confusion can create feelings of disorientation, making it difficult for individuals to focus on immediate tasks that require clarity of thought.

Anger is a common emotional response to trauma. People often find themselves overwhelmed with frustration and exasperation, partly due to the ordeal they've been through. Sometimes, this anger remains bottled up inside, leading to feelings of shame and guilt. In other cases, it is externalised and can manifest as hostility and irrational outbursts.

Depression is another emotional response that frequently lingers after a traumatic event. People may feel disconnected from their own lives as if nothing holds significance anymore. It can lead to difficulties with eating, sleeping, and even the most mundane daily activities.

Transitioning from the emotional effects of trauma to 'self-rejection,' it is crucial to recognise that self-rejection is a complex concept with intricate connections to the aftermath of trauma. Self-rejection involves the act of emotionally or physically denying aspects of oneself, often rooted in feelings of unworthiness and low self-esteem. These sentiments can be traced back to childhood experiences, including criticism from parents, teachers, or peers. Additionally, self-rejection may stem from setting unrealistic self-expectations and engaging in negative self-talk.

The emotional responses following trauma, such as fear, anxiety, shock, confusion, anger, and depression, can contribute to the development of self-rejection. Individuals who have undergone traumatic experiences may internalise the negative emotions associated with trauma, leading to a distorted self-perception. The overwhelming fear and anxiety may translate into a belief in one's unworthiness, fostering an environment where self-rejection becomes a coping mechanism.

The persistent shock and confusion post-trauma may contribute to feelings of detachment from oneself, creating a void that self-rejection attempts to fill. Anger, whether internalised or externalised, can manifest as self-directed frustration, reinforcing the notion of being undeserving. Depression, with its profound impact on daily functioning, further exacerbates feelings of self-rejection, as individuals struggle to find meaning and significance in their own lives.

Understanding the roots of self-rejection in childhood experiences highlights the enduring impact of early criticisms and negative feedback. Trauma may amplify these childhood wounds, deepening the sense of unworthiness. Setting unrealistic self-expectations, possibly fuelled by societal pressure or unrealistic standards, becomes another avenue through which self-rejection takes root. Negative self-talk, often a product of internalised trauma-related emotions, serves to perpetuate the cycle of self-rejection by reinforcing negative beliefs about one's worth.

In essence, the emotional aftermath of trauma lays the groundwork for self-rejection by influencing perceptions of worthiness, distorting self-image, and fostering negative beliefs. Traumatic experiences- such as abuse, violence, and neglect, play a significant role in the development of self-rejection. They intensify feelings of shame, guilt, and unworthiness. In the aftermath of such experiences, individuals often struggle with self-acceptance. Overcoming self-rejection can be especially challenging after enduring trauma.

Identity, encompassing a sense of self-worth and belonging to specific communities, families, or cultures, plays a pivotal role in shaping an individual's experience of self-rejection. This intricate connection is influenced by various factors, including prejudice, discrimination, cultural norms, and societal expectations, all of which unfold within the realm of psychological dynamics.

Individuals often derive a significant portion of their self-worth from their cultural identity. Cultural values, traditions, and norms contribute to a person's sense of belonging and self-esteem. However, when cultural identity is marginalised or devalued, it can become a source of self-rejection. Experiencing prejudice or discrimination based on cultural background may lead individuals to internalise negative beliefs about themselves, fostering feelings of unworthiness.

The sense of belonging to communities, families, or other social groups is integral to forming one's identity. Positive connections within these groups can enhance self-esteem and reinforce a sense of worthiness. Conversely, rejection or exclusion within these social spheres can contribute to self-rejection. Psychological studies highlight the impact of social exclusion on self-perception, showing that feelings of rejection trigger negative emotional responses and undermine one's sense of self.

Prejudice and discrimination, whether based on race, ethnicity, gender, or other factors, are potent contributors to self-rejection. When individuals face bias or unfair treatment, it can lead to the internalisation of negative stereotypes and beliefs. Psychologically, this internalisation can manifest as a diminished sense of self-worth. The emotional toll of discrimination may compound the effects of trauma and contribute to a cycle of self-rejection.

Cultural norms and societal expectations shape individuals' behaviours and self-perceptions. Conforming to these norms may enhance one's sense of acceptance and belonging, positively influencing self-worth. However, when individuals deviate from cultural expectations or fail to meet societal standards, it can result in feelings of inadequacy and self-rejection.

Understanding the cause-and-effect cycle of self-rejection is crucial. Individuals who grapple with self-rejection may withdraw from social situations, turning inward and exacerbating feelings of isolation. This, in turn, leads to more self-rejecting thoughts and actions, creating a self-perpetuating cycle that can be challenging to break free from once it takes hold.

The impact of self-rejection- extends beyond individual suffering. It can strain relationships, hindering individuals from accepting love and support from others. Opening up to others and being vulnerable becomes a monumental challenge, particularly in close personal relationships.

Additionally, the inability to control emotions often results from self-rejection. Engaging in self-destructive internal dialogue may lead to unmanageable feelings of low self-worth, depression, and anxiety. Individuals who struggle with self-rejection, often marked by low self-esteem, are more likely to engage in risky behaviours such as substance abuse, as a way to cope with the negative emotions they experience.

The impact of criticism from family, friends, or society at large on self-rejection is profound and complex. Negative comments about one's physical appearance, personality, or any aspect perceived as a reflection of oneself can deeply influence self-perception, with lasting effects that extend beyond the immediate moment of criticism. Consistent criticism acts as a potent force in eroding an individual's self-esteem. Psychologically, self-esteem reflects one's overall subjective emotional evaluation of their own worth. When subjected to ongoing criticism, individuals internalise negative assessments, leading to a gradual erosion of their perception of self-worth. This erosion is not merely a surface-level impact; it penetrates deep into the core of an individual's psyche, shaping their self-concept.

The intricate relationship between perfectionism and self-rejection delves into the depths of individuals who set rigorous standards for themselves, often fuelled by a desire for external validation or an internal need to meet an unrealistic ideal. This journey begins with the establishment of lofty expectations. The subsequent disappointment, when these expectations inevitably fall short, becomes a breeding ground for self-rejection.

Perfectionists tend to set standards that surpass reasonable and achievable goals. These unrealistic expectations create a perpetual cycle of striving for an elusive perfection. When these standards are not met, individuals may internalise the perceived failure as evidence of their inherent inadequacy. This internal dialogue, rooted in the psychology of self-perception, contributes to a deep-seated belief in one's unworthiness. The toll of unmet expectations often manifests in a cascade of negative thoughts and behaviours. Individuals may engage in self-criticism, harsh judgment, and an intensified fear of failure. These negative cognitions fuel self-rejection as the gap between the idealised self and the perceived, imperfect self widens. Behaviours may include avoidance of challenges, procrastination, or a relentless pursuit of unattainable goals, all driven by the psychological need to rectify the perceived inadequacy. Perfectionism, at its core, influences self-esteem and identity formation. Self-esteem reflects an individual's overall subjective evaluation of their own worth. The relentless pursuit of perfection, coupled with the constant disappointment of falling short, can erode self-esteem. This erosion, intertwined with the psychological construct of identity, creates a dissonance between the perceived self and the idealised self, fostering an environment conducive to self-rejection.

Perfectionists often harbour a profound fear of evaluation by others. This fear stems from the belief that one's worth is contingent upon meeting external standards. The perpetual pursuit of perfection becomes a means of seeking external validation. The fear of falling short of these external standards intensifies the psychological cycle of self-rejection.

The interplay between perfectionism and self-rejection creates a self-reinforcing cycle. The pursuit of an unattainable ideal leads to repeated disappointments and negative self-appraisals. These, in turn, fuel the need for perfection as a coping mechanism to alleviate the perceived inadequacy.

Individuals grappling with low self-esteem often find themselves harbouring a deep-seated dislike for various aspects of themselves. This self-disdain extends beyond mere dissatisfaction, manifesting as a hyper-focus on perceived flaws, whether in physical appearance or character traits. In their internal narrative, individuals with low self-esteem may perpetuate a false belief system, convincing themselves that they are inherently inadequate and do not measure up to the societal or external standards imposed upon them. This pervasive sense of inadequacy becomes a fertile ground for the cultivation of self-rejection. The individuals, enveloped in the shadows of low self-esteem, internalise the negative perceptions and judgments, creating an ongoing cycle of self-disparagement. The relentless comparison to external standards and the constant fear of falling short contribute to the reinforcing loop of self-rejection. Low self-esteem, acting as a catalyst for self-rejection, not only impacts how individuals perceive themselves but also influences their interactions with the world. It becomes a lens through which they interpret experiences, often distorting reality to align with their negative self-image. This distorted lens may hinder personal and professional growth, as individuals may avoid opportunities, relationships, and challenges due to an ingrained belief that they are inherently unworthy.

Traumatic experiences, such as abuse and bullying, possess a profound capacity to sow the seeds of self-rejection in the minds of those who endure them. These individuals often find themselves grappling not only with the tangible repercussions of the traumatic events but also with the insidious aftermath that infiltrates their sense of self-worth. One of the detrimental outcomes of traumatic experiences is the internalisation of blame. Victims may erroneously assume responsibility for the traumatic events, fostering a distorted belief that they are somehow at fault for the hardships they faced. This internalised blame becomes a toxic undercurrent, permeating their self-perception and contributing to a deep-seated sense of unworthiness. In the crucible of traumatic experiences, individuals may find themselves caught in a cycle of self-loathing. The emotional and psychological wounds inflicted during these events may fester, creating a persistent narrative that they are undeserving of love, respect, or happiness. This self-loathing is often exacerbated by internalised blame, creating a self-reinforcing cycle that becomes increasingly challenging to break. Moreover, the impact of traumatic experiences on self-rejection is enduring. The scars left by abuse and bullying extend far beyond the immediate aftermath of the events. Individuals may carry the emotional weight of these experiences for an extended period, making it a formidable challenge to overcome the clutches of self-rejection.

The pervasive nature of self-rejection following traumatic experiences can manifest in various ways. It may hinder individuals from forming healthy relationships, as they may struggle to trust others or believe they are deserving of genuine connection. Additionally, it can impede personal and professional growth, as the internalised belief of unworthiness may sabotage opportunities for advancement or success.

The repercussions of self-rejection extend across the intricate tapestry of our existence, permeating our physical, mental, and spiritual realms. Self-rejection takes a toll on the physical body by inducing stress responses that compromise the immune system. This heightened state of stress contributes to a range of physical ailments, including digestive issues, headaches, and fatigue. The confluence of stress and physical symptoms is further compounded by the emotional burden of self-rejection, leading to challenges such as disrupted sleep patterns, difficulty concentrating, and muscle tension. The negative self-image cultivated through self-rejection thus initiates a cycle of stress, weakened immunity, and associated physical manifestations.

Mentally, the consequences of self-rejection are palpable. The act of rejecting oneself opens the floodgates to self-critical thoughts and beliefs, fostering a downward spiral of negative self-perception. Individuals grappling with self-rejection often shoulder self-blame for perceived failures, nurturing a pervasive sense of low self-esteem, worthlessness, and diminished self-confidence. This mental landscape impedes the capacity to set boundaries, make decisions, and form healthy relationships. The self-doubt accompanying self-rejection becomes a breeding ground for anxiety and depression, establishing a harmful cycle of negative self-talk that hampers overall well-being and stifles personal growth.

Spiritual well-being, too, is not immune to the reverberations of self-rejection. When individuals reject their own self-image, a profound disconnection ensues—both from their inner sense of purpose and the broader world. This disconnection extends to spiritual beliefs and values, fostering feelings of unworthiness and a deep-seated belief that love and acceptance are undeserved. The spiritual consequences of self-rejection manifest as an enduring sense of hopelessness, helplessness, and despair. This dissonance impedes the ability to find meaning and purpose in life, intensifying the emotional and psychological challenges associated with self-rejection. The profound interplay of physical, mental, and spiritual consequences underscores the imperative of addressing self-rejection holistically, with compassion and a commitment to fostering self-acceptance.

Breaking free from the cycle of self-rejection stands as a pivotal juncture for personal growth and overall well-being. To combat the insidious traits associated with self-rejection, the journey commences with the crucial step of recognising and challenging the negative beliefs internalised about oneself. These beliefs often find their origins in past experiences, environmental messages, or self-imposed thoughts, undermining self-esteem and impeding progress toward personal goals.

Self-rejection traits, being often blind spots in our self-awareness, demand identification and confrontation for individuals to advance in life and foster healthier self-perceptions. Confronting the negative thoughts and feelings associated with self-rejection is challenging but fundamental for personal growth. A healthy self-dialogue that encourages and motivates, coupled with the acknowledgment and celebration of unique qualities, strengths, and achievements, becomes a counterforce to the negative beliefs that perpetuate self-rejection.

Surrounding oneself with a supportive and nurturing environment stands as another critical aspect of addressing self-rejection. Supportive friends and family offer a safe space for individuals to challenge negative thoughts and develop a robust sense of self-worth. In the arsenal against self-rejection, mindfulness and self-care emerge as essential components. Mindfulness, rooted in being fully present in the moment, enables individuals to recognise and navigate their thoughts and feelings. Engaging in activities that bring joy and a sense of accomplishment becomes a potent tool for reducing stress levels and boosting self-confidence, fostering a holistic improvement in overall well-being.

Confronting and overcoming self-rejection requires individuals to identify cognitive distortions and replace them with more accurate thoughts and beliefs. This process demands self-awareness and an understanding of the roots of self-rejection within one's life. While living with emotional blind spots, self-regulating emotions becomes a formidable challenge. These blind spots can obscure the true source of emotional reactions, leading individuals to focus on surface-level issues or external triggers. Recognising these underlying factors and effectively managing emotions necessitates heightened awareness and understanding.

Once emotional blind spots are recognised and addressed, individuals embark on the journey of self-regulation. This involves cultivating self-compassion and patience while learning to manage emotions effectively. Recognising that emotional self-regulation is an ongoing journey is essential, as it may take time and effort to fully develop these skills. The impact of self-rejection is not confined to the individual; it reverberates through generations. Unchecked self-rejection can become a pattern transmitted to the next generation, shaping the emotional landscape of our children. The beliefs and coping mechanisms developed by individuals in response to self-rejection can influence their parenting styles, inadvertently passing down patterns of negative self-perception. Thus, the journey to break free from self-rejection is not only a personal endeavour but a generational legacy, influencing the well-being and mindset of the children that follow.

Chapter 6
The Impact of Feeling Undeserved and Breaking the Victimhood Cycle

The implications of feeling undeserved extend beyond the individual, leaving an indelible mark on the intergenerational landscape. This section explores how the cycle of unmerited if unbroken, can influence the values and perspectives passed on to the next generation.

Parents, as primary influencers, play a pivotal role in shaping their children's worldview. If individuals harbour a sense of being unmerited, there is a risk that these narratives will be transmitted to their offspring. Children absorb not only explicit teachings but also the subtle cues and attitudes displayed within the family unit, potentially perpetuating the cycle of unworthiness.

The Emotional Impact of Feeling Unmerited

Feeling undeserved casts a heavy emotional burden on individuals, infiltrating every aspect of their lives. Let's delve into the intricate tapestry of emotions that often accompanies this sense of unmerited, exploring the nuances of self-doubt, inadequacy, and resentment.

When individuals grapple with the belief that they are undeserving, a complex interplay of emotions takes root, with self-doubt emerging as a constant and insidious companion. This self-doubt becomes a formidable force, eroding confidence in one's abilities and intrinsic value. The psychological phenomenon commonly known as imposter syndrome often surfaces, where achievements are consistently undermined. Those affected attribute success to external factors, deflecting acknowledgment of personal competence. This perpetual shadow of unreservedness casts a paralysing effect on every accomplishment, creating a hindrance to both personal and professional growth.

In tandem with self-doubt, the feeling of inadequacy establishes its roots in the individual's psyche. Those who perceive themselves as undeserving internalise a pervasive sense of insufficiency, firmly believing they fall short of societal or personal standards. This feeling of not measuring up leads to chronic stress, anxiety, and a persistent fear of judgment. In the professional realm, inadequacy may act as a barrier to career advancement, hindering individuals from actively pursuing opportunities or expressing innovative ideas. On a personal level, this sense of inadequacy impacts relationships, as a lingering fear of not being 'enough' may lead to withdrawal or avoidance of social interactions.

Delving into psychological science, these manifestations of self-doubt and inadequacy align with research on cognitive distortions. Cognitive distortions are irrational thought patterns that reinforce negative beliefs about oneself. The distorted thinking associated with feeling underserved can create a self-fulfilling prophecy, perpetuating a cycle of negative thoughts and behaviours.

The emotional landscape of feeling unmerited is often marked by resentment—a deep-seated bitterness towards those perceived as more fortunate or privileged. Psychologically, this resentment may be linked to social comparison theory, where individuals evaluate themselves against others, leading to feelings of inferiority. Left unexamined, this resentment can fester, evolving into a toxic force in personal and professional relationships.

In the workplace, this resentment may manifest as dissatisfaction with colleagues or supervisors receiving what is perceived as undue recognition or opportunities. Psychologically, this aligns with equity theory, where individuals compare their inputs (effort, contributions) and outputs (rewards, recognition) to those of others. In personal relationships, resentment can strain connections as individuals grapple with bitterness towards those believed to possess more advantages or validation.

Left unchecked, the amalgamation of self-doubt, inadequacy, and resentment contributes to a perpetual cycle of victimhood—a psychological state where individuals passively accept negative circumstances, attributing their struggles solely to external factors. This aligns with learned helplessness theory, where repeated negative experiences lead individuals to believe they have no control over their situation, fostering a sense of victimhood.

Exploring the intricate relationship between deservingness and happiness unveils a profound psychological journey. Psychologically, deservingness is tightly woven into self-worth and self-esteem. Studies in positive psychology underscore that acknowledging one's deservingness correlates with elevated self-compassion, positive self-regard, and overall subjective well-being.

As individuals undergo a transformative shift in recognising their deservingness, a profound psychological impact ensues. This shift involves challenging negative self-talk and adopting affirming beliefs, often facilitated through cognitive-behavioural interventions utilised in therapy. This reframing of self-perception lays the groundwork for increased resilience, better mental health, and a heightened sense of overall well-being.

The positive psychological consequences of deservingness extend to the realm of emotions and purpose. Individuals embracing deservingness naturally cultivate positive emotions, linked to resilience, improved physical health, and greater life satisfaction. This shift also fosters a deeper sense of purpose, influencing goal-setting, passion pursuit, and an overall enhanced fulfilment in life. The newfound self-affirmation arising from recognising deservingness contributes to an increased capacity for joy. Positive psychology emphasises the importance of savouring positive experiences, and individuals who feel deserving are more likely to engage in this practice. Complementary to the cultivation of deservingness, mindfulness-based interventions, such as Acceptance and Commitment Therapy (ACT), facilitate the acknowledgment and acceptance of thoughts and feelings without judgment, ultimately paving the way for positive behavioural change.

Breaking the undeserving blind spot emerges as a powerful catalyst for personal happiness and contentment. This intricate process involves dismantling deeply ingrained beliefs through therapeutic approaches grounded in mindfulness and acceptance. Additionally, the role of gratitude intersects with deservingness, encouraging individuals to cultivate gratitude for their strengths, achievements, and positive experiences, thus enhancing overall well-being and life satisfaction. Acknowledging the undeserving blind spot within family dynamics initiates a transformative process requiring a collective understanding of historical patterns. Family members must delve into shared experiences and values that have shaped beliefs about deservingness over time. Simultaneously, gaining insight into how these narratives impact relationships across generations is crucial for fostering empathy and compassion among family members.

This acknowledgment extends beyond mere awareness; it involves a shared commitment to instigate change. Family members must collectively agree that breaking free from the undeserving cycle is a worthwhile and achievable goal. This commitment becomes a unifying force, aligning the family towards a common purpose of fostering healthier connections and dismantling negative beliefs associated with being underserving.

Active listening emerges as a catalyst for change during these family discussions. Each family member commits to genuinely hearing and understanding the experiences and viewpoints of others. This practice cultivates empathy and lays the groundwork for mutual respect. Techniques such as reflective listening enhance the effectiveness of these dialogues. Creating an environment where every family member feels empowered to express their thoughts and concerns is paramount. Encouraging assertiveness and validating individual experiences contribute to a culture of openness. This empowerment enables family members to actively participate in reshaping the narrative around deservingness, fostering a sense of agency in the collective journey towards positive change.

Acknowledging the undeserving blind spot is an ongoing process that requires continuous re-evaluation and adaptation. Family dynamics evolve, and so too should the collective understanding of deservingness. Regular check-ins, reflective practices, and a commitment to adapt as needed ensure that the journey toward breaking free from the undeserving cycle remains dynamic, responsive, and effective. However, if parents leave the undeserving trait unchecked and fail to embrace the catalysts for a mindset of empowerment, several negative consequences may unfold in the lives of their children and future generations.

Individuals may grapple with low self-esteem and confidence in the absence of self-worth promotion and positive beliefs about deservingness. Without affirmations and acknowledgment of inherent value, a persistent sense of inadequacy may hinder their ability to navigate life's challenges with confidence. The lack of educational interventions and resilience cultivation can leave individuals ill-equipped to face life's inevitable challenges. Insufficient emotional intelligence and coping skills may result in difficulties bouncing back from setbacks, potentially leading to heightened stress, anxiety, and a diminished capacity to overcome adversity.

Open communication within families plays a crucial role in fostering understanding and unity. Without this foundation, interpersonal relationships may suffer, as individuals struggle to express thoughts and emotions. This can lead to misunderstandings and strained connections within the family unit and, consequently, in broader social interactions.

The absence of initiatives to counteract undeserving beliefs allows negative narratives to persist, influencing decision-making, goal-setting, and overall life satisfaction. This reinforcement of negative beliefs can create a self-fulfilling prophecy, limiting individuals from reaching their full potential.

Unchecked undeserving beliefs have the potential to be transmitted to subsequent generations, perpetuating a cycle where children inherit and internalise the same negative narratives about their worth. This generational transmission could contribute to a sustained pattern of unfulfilled potential and hindered well-being within the family lineage. Educational interventions not only provide knowledge but also contribute to emotional well-being. Without these interventions, individuals may lack the emotional intelligence to understand and manage their feelings effectively. This deficit in emotional well-being can lead to heightened stress, difficulties in forming meaningful connections, and an overall diminished quality of life. The absence of a holistic approach to empowerment denies individuals opportunities for personal growth. Educational interventions, open communication, and the promotion of self-worth create a synergistic environment that fosters continuous development. Without these catalysts, individuals may miss out on crucial chances for self-discovery, learning, and personal fulfilment.

In essence, if parents neglect to address the undeserving trait and implement catalysts for empowerment, they risk perpetuating a cycle of diminished self-worth, limited resilience, and strained relationships within their family. The implications may extend to future generations, impacting the overall well-being and potential of individuals within the family lineage. This underscores the importance of actively engaging in strategies that foster empowerment, resilience, and a positive sense of self-worth to ensure a healthier and more fulfilling trajectory for the generations to come.

Chapter 7
Overcoming Our Blind Spots:
Strategies for Self-Reflection and Improvement

Have you ever found yourself surprised by feedback from someone close, like a friend or co-worker? Perhaps they brought up a habit or flaw in your work that you weren't aware of. Though these situations can be uncomfortable, they offer valuable opportunities for personal development and self-discovery.

Blind spots are aspects of ourselves that we're unaware of or don't fully understand, such as prejudices, routines, and behavioural patterns. These blind spots can limit our ability to collaborate effectively, communicate clearly, and build meaningful connections with others. When we're unaware of these blind spots, we risk unintentionally causing harm to ourselves and those around us. Recognising our blind spots can indeed be a challenging endeavour. Let's be honest – who enjoys being pointed out or criticised? When someone brings attention to something we hadn't noticed or feels so ingrained in our personalities that it becomes a part of who we are, it's only natural to feel defensive or resistant to criticism. Therefore, it becomes crucial to approach this process with an open mind and a sincere willingness to learn. To improve our interactions with others, our performance at work, and ourselves, there are some techniques for recognising and addressing our blind spots. Here are a few examples:

Self-Awareness:
Recognising and Understanding Our Blind Spots

Self-awareness plays a pivotal role in our personal development, particularly when it comes to recognising and understanding our blind spots. These blind spots, encompassing biases, routines, and behavioural patterns, often operate beneath our conscious awareness. However, by bringing them into our awareness, we gain the power to take proactive steps towards addressing and mitigating their impact.

Self-awareness, in its essence, entails the ability to not only recognise but also comprehend our thoughts, emotions, behaviours, and tendencies. It goes beyond a superficial understanding of our strengths and weaknesses; it involves a profound exploration of the potential blind spots that may impede our growth. By shedding light on these blind spots, we enhance our consciousness of ourselves, paving the way for intentional and transformative actions.

The journey of self-awareness involves a dynamic process of introspection, observation, and reflection. It requires us to delve into the intricate layers of our psyche, uncovering hidden biases and habitual responses. Acknowledging both the positive and challenging aspects of ourselves fosters a holistic self-awareness that forms the foundation for personal growth.

A critical facet of self-awareness involves the acknowledgment and understanding of our biases. Biases are latent beliefs or attitudes residing in our subconscious about specific groups of people. These biases, whether related to race, gender, or other characteristics, possess the potential to shape our thoughts, actions, and decisions subtly. Unearthing these biases is a key step in cultivating a heightened self-awareness. It requires a deliberate examination of our own perceptions and attitudes, often unveiling implicit prejudices we may not be consciously aware of. These biases, if left unexamined, can permeate various aspects of our lives, influencing how we perceive others and impacting our interactions.

The recognition of biases is not a condemnation but an opportunity for growth. By bringing these biases to light, we empower ourselves to confront and challenge them. This awareness opens the door to intentional efforts to overcome biases, fostering a mindset of inclusivity and fairness. Overcoming biases demands a commitment to continuous self-reflection and education. It involves actively seeking to understand and dismantle preconceived notions that may cloud our judgment. This process requires humility and openness to change, as we strive to reshape our perspectives and cultivate a more nuanced understanding of the diverse individuals with whom we interact.

Delving into the realm of self-awareness extends beyond recognising biases; it also encompasses understanding our daily routines and behavioural patterns. These habitual actions often weave themselves into the fabric of our lives subtly, becoming ingrained before we are even aware. Unconscious adherence to routines can inadvertently hinder personal growth by creating a comfort zone that limits exploration and novelty.

The realisation of these patterns demands a heightened level of mindfulness. It entails a deliberate examination of our daily activities, acknowledging the repetitive nature of certain behaviours that may be hindering our growth potential. Identifying these routines becomes a catalyst for self-discovery, as it sheds light on areas where we might be stagnating or missing opportunities for development.

Conscious awareness of routines opens the door to intentional change. Recognising where we may be stuck or complacent empowers us to break free from the confines of our comfort zones. It serves as a call to action, prompting us to explore new avenues, try different approaches, and embrace challenges that lie beyond the familiar territory of our routines.

Breaking out of established patterns requires a willingness to embrace discomfort and uncertainty. This process is an opportunity for self-exploration and the cultivation of resilience. As we venture beyond the boundaries of our habitual behaviours, we create space for personal evolution and the acquisition of diverse skills and perspectives.

Self-awareness proves to be a multifaceted asset, extending its benefits beyond personal growth into the realms of relationships, work, and various aspects of life. The profound understanding of our thoughts, emotions, and behaviours not only catalyses individual development but also significantly influences our interactions with others.

In the context of relationships, self-awareness serves as a compass, enabling us to navigate the intricate dynamics with a heightened sense of understanding. Recognising patterns in our interactions allows us to pinpoint areas of potential conflict or misunderstanding, fostering an environment where we can proactively address and resolve issues. Moreover, by acknowledging our biases and blind spots, we cultivate empathy towards others, enhancing our capacity for nuanced communication and fostering the strength of our relationships.

Within the workplace, self-awareness assumes a pivotal role in effective leadership and teamwork. Leaders endowed with self-awareness possess a comprehensive understanding of their own strengths and weaknesses, allowing them to navigate challenges with a strategic mindset. This awareness extends to team dynamics, as leaders recognise and leverage the diverse strengths and weaknesses of their team members to achieve collective objectives. Employees, too, benefit from self-awareness, using it as a compass to identify areas for improvement and actively pursuing the development of their skills and capabilities.

Furthermore, self-awareness acts as a valuable tool for emotional and behavioural management, particularly in stressful or challenging situations. Recognition of personal triggers and patterns empowers individuals to develop coping strategies and make conscious choices in responding positively and constructively.

In essence, self-awareness emerges as an invaluable skill that permeates all facets of life. The conscious understanding of oneself becomes a catalyst for positive change, facilitating growth on both personal and professional fronts. It enhances the quality of relationships, fosters effective collaboration in the workplace, and equips individuals with the tools to manage their emotions and behaviours constructively. While self-awareness is an ongoing journey, a deliberate effort to cultivate it ensures that we continually evolve towards becoming the best versions of ourselves.

Communication: Overcoming Blind Spots for Clearer Communication

Blind spots have the potential to hinder our ability to communicate effectively. For example, if we remain unaware of our body language, we might inadvertently convey misleading signals to others. By acknowledging and addressing these blind spots, we can improve our relationships and elevate our communication skills.

Successful relationships, be they personal or professional, hinge on effective communication. This encompasses not just the content of our messages but also how we convey them and our ability to listen. Yet, our blind spots, those elements of ourselves and our communication approach that elude our awareness can impede this process.

A prevalent blind spot in communication lies in nonverbal cues, encompassing body language, facial expressions, and tone of voice. Often, we are not fully conscious of the signals we emit, leading to potential misunderstandings. For instance, an inadvertent display of disinterest or defensiveness in our body language can contradict the intended message we seek to convey.

Effectively addressing this blind spot necessitates a heightened awareness of our nonverbal communication. Self-observation proves invaluable, and leveraging tools like video or audio recordings allows us to scrutinize our interactions for subtle cues that might hinder effective communication. Through this process, we can identify areas where our nonverbal signals may not align with our verbal expressions.

Moreover, seeking feedback from trusted individuals becomes a valuable strategy for illuminating these blind spots. External perspectives can provide nuanced insights into aspects of our nonverbal communication that we might overlook. This collaborative approach to self-improvement ensures a more comprehensive understanding of how our nonverbal cues impact our communication dynamics.

Yet another frequent blind spot in communication lies in active listening. Despite many of us believing we excel in this skill, the reality often reveals a different story. We might find ourselves more engaged in formulating our responses than in truly comprehending the speaker's message. This diversion can result in overlooking crucial information and a failure to fully grasp the speaker's perspective.

To address and rectify this blind spot, we can adopt active listening techniques. This involves dedicating our complete attention to the speaker, asking clarifying questions, and summarising what we've heard to ensure an accurate understanding. Practising active listening not only enhances our communication abilities but also serves as a tangible demonstration of our respect for the speaker.

The inability to express assertiveness can have deep-seated psychological aspects that impact an individual's communication and overall well-being. When someone struggles with assertiveness, it may stem from various factors, including fear of rejection, a desire to avoid conflict, low self-esteem, or a history of negative experiences when expressing themselves.

For instance, an individual who fears rejection might hesitate to assert their needs or boundaries, anticipating negative reactions from others. Similarly, someone with low self-esteem might struggle to believe that their needs are valid or deserve consideration.

Avoiding confrontation and prioritising others' needs over their own can be coping mechanisms developed over time to navigate these psychological challenges. It might provide a temporary sense of safety but can lead to long-term dissatisfaction and unfulfilled personal needs.

Addressing the psychological aspects of assertiveness often involves self-reflection and, in some cases, seeking support from mental health professionals. Developing a healthy sense of self-worth, challenging negative beliefs, and learning effective communication strategies are crucial components of building assertiveness.

Cultivating assertiveness skills is not just about improving communication; it's also a journey towards building healthier relationships and fostering a more positive self-image. Through recognising and actively addressing the aspects that hinder assertiveness, individuals can embark on a transformative process that positively influences various aspects of their lives.

Collaboration: Fostering Effective Collaboration by Overcoming Blind Spots

Navigating a group setting poses challenges when blind spots hinder successful collaboration. For example, failing to acknowledge biases may lead to the unintentional exclusion or dismissal of certain team members or their ideas. Awareness of these blind spots is crucial for enhanced collaboration and improved outcomes.

Collaboration is a vital component in different facets of life, extending from workplace teamwork to cooperative endeavours in personal relationships. Yet, blind spots have the potential to impede our capacity for successful collaboration. Here are several common blind spots that can affect collaboration, along with strategies to overcome them:

- **Overconfidence** in a collaborative setting can be a significant hindrance, as it involves an individual overestimating their abilities or knowledge. This psychological aspect may stem from various sources, such as a need for validation, a desire to project competence, or a fear of appearing vulnerable. Overconfident individuals may perceive their way as the only correct one, leading to a reluctance to consider others' input or dismiss valuable contributions from team members.

Psychologically, overconfidence often masks insecurities or a fear of inadequacy. The individual may feel compelled to project an image of unwavering certainty to protect their self-esteem. This defensive mechanism can result in a lack of receptivity to alternative viewpoints, limiting the potential for collaborative synergy.

To address overconfidence, fostering humility becomes essential. Cultivating humility involves acknowledging one's limitations and recognising that no one possesses all the answers. Embracing a willingness to learn from others and valuing diverse perspectives can be transformative. This shift involves reframing one's self-perception from a need to be right to a genuine curiosity about different viewpoints.

- **Resistance to Change:** In a workplace setting, resistance to change can have profound implications that affect both individual and collective dynamics. Individuals who resist change may fear the potential disruption to their established routines, viewing the unknown as a source of stress and discomfort. The desire for stability and control can be particularly pronounced in a professional context, where perceived competence is closely tied to one's ability to navigate familiar processes.

  Moreover, in the workplace, resistance to change may be fuelled by concerns about job security, the fear of being overshadowed by new technologies, or a reluctance to step outside one's comfort zone. The workplace environment often amplifies these psychological factors, as individuals may feel the need to prove their competence and reliability in the face of organisational shifts.

Addressing this resistance involves not only fostering a growth mindset but also creating a workplace culture that values adaptability. Encouraging open communication and providing forums for employees to express their concerns can contribute to a safe environment where individuals feel heard and supported during periods of change.

In personal life, resistance to change can manifest in various ways, impacting relationships, lifestyle choices, and personal development. Factors such as fear of the unknown, attachment to comfort zones, or the desire for routine can influence an individual's resistance to change in their personal life.

For example, someone may resist changing a daily routine out of fear that it will disrupt their sense of balance or security. In relationships, resistance to change may be linked to a reluctance to confront challenging issues or a fear of the potential consequences of personal growth.

Overcoming this resistance in personal life requires a similar shift in mindset—a willingness to embrace change as an opportunity for learning and development. Cultivating flexibility and openness can lead to a more fulfilling personal life, where individuals are better equipped to navigate challenges and pursue personal growth.

- **Lack of Empathy:** In a professional context, a lack of empathy can have profound implications for collaboration and teamwork. The workplace is a dynamic environment where effective communication and understanding are paramount. When empathy is lacking, team members may struggle to connect on a personal level, hindering the development of a cohesive and supportive work culture.

  From a professional standpoint, an individual's inability to empathise may manifest in challenges such as difficulty understanding the perspectives of colleagues, an inability to navigate conflicts with sensitivity, or a failure to recognise the emotional needs of team members. These deficiencies can impede the overall effectiveness of collaborative efforts, impacting productivity, morale, and the quality of work relationships.

Moreover, in professional settings, a lack of empathy can hinder leadership effectiveness. Leaders who are unable to understand and respond to the needs and concerns of their team may struggle to inspire trust and loyalty. This can lead to a disengaged and less motivated workforce, ultimately affecting the success of projects and organisational goals.

In personal relationships, a deficiency in empathy can strain connections and hinder the development of meaningful bonds. Individuals who struggle to empathise may find it challenging to navigate emotional landscapes, leading to misunderstandings, conflicts, and a lack of emotional support.

From a personal standpoint, a lack of empathy can contribute to difficulties in establishing and maintaining close relationships. Friends, family members, and romantic partners may feel unheard or unacknowledged, eroding the foundation of trust and mutual understanding. In personal relationships, empathy serves as a bridge that fosters emotional connection and intimacy.

Personal Development: Embracing Growth Through Blind Spot Awareness

Personal development depends on our ability to identify our blind spots. We can identify areas for development and work to become our best selves by having a better understanding of who we are. Blind spots in personal development are areas of our lives and selves that we may not fully comprehend or areas where our understanding is limited. These blind spots can hinder our personal growth and development, preventing us from becoming the best versions of ourselves. Here are some ways in which blind spot awareness can enhance personal development:

- **Recognising Self-Limiting Beliefs:** Blind spots often manifest as self-limiting beliefs, negative convictions about ourselves that hinder our potential. These beliefs are deeply ingrained and influenced by various psychological factors.

  Early experiences and conditioning during childhood play a significant role in shaping self-perception. Negative feedback or experiences may lead to internalised self-limiting beliefs, such as feelings of inadequacy. Social and cultural influences contribute as well, setting unrealistic standards that individuals may feel they fall short of, and fostering limiting beliefs.

  Negative self-talk, a harsh internal dialogue, reinforces these beliefs. It can stem from external criticisms, creating a continuous negative narrative that erodes self-confidence. The fear of failure or rejection further solidifies self-limiting beliefs, causing individuals to avoid risks or opportunities due to anticipated negative outcomes.

  Constant comparison with others, often fuelled by societal norms or social media, contributes to feelings of inadequacy. Perceiving others as more successful may lead to the adoption of limiting beliefs about one's own capabilities. Additionally, a perceived lack of control over life circumstances can foster these beliefs, undermining confidence in one's ability to effect positive change. Individuals with a fixed mindset, assuming abilities are innate and unchangeable, may be more prone to self-limiting beliefs. This mindset fosters the belief that improvement or success is unattainable. Overcoming these beliefs requires cultivating self-awareness and challenging ingrained thinking patterns.

  Strategies such as cognitive-behavioural techniques, positive affirmations, and reframing negative thoughts can be effective. Seeking support from therapists, coaches, or mentors guides in navigating and transforming self-limiting beliefs. Recognising the psychological roots empowers individuals to break free from constraints, fostering personal growth, resilience, and increased self-confidence.

- **Enhancing Self-Awareness:** Enhancing self-awareness is a crucial aspect of personal development. At its core, self-awareness involves a deep understanding of one's own thoughts, emotions, behaviours, and tendencies. Blind spot awareness is a valuable tool in this pursuit, as it sheds light on aspects of ourselves that were previously hidden or overlooked. One significant contribution of blind spot awareness to self-awareness is the revelation of hidden strengths and weaknesses. Often, these strengths and weaknesses are obscured by our unconscious behaviours or by the assumptions we make about ourselves. Identifying these hidden aspects allows us to leverage our strengths more effectively and address our weaknesses proactively. Informed decision-making is another benefit of cultivating blind spot awareness. When we are conscious of our blind spots, we are less likely to be influenced by unconscious biases or habitual patterns. This awareness empowers us to make choices that align with our values and contribute to our overall well-being.

- **Breaking Patterns of Behaviour:** Blind spots in personal development often manifest as recurring patterns of behaviour that hinder our growth goals. These patterns, operating at a subconscious level, may be influenced by cognitive biases, defence mechanisms, past trauma, fear of vulnerability, and habitual responses. For example, avoidance of difficult conversations may result from a blind spot related to communication. Recognising these patterns is crucial for breaking free from unproductive behaviours. Psychological factors like cognitive biases and defence mechanisms contribute to the formation of blind spots. Past trauma or conditioning, fear of vulnerability, and habitual responses further shape these patterns.

- **Developing a Growth Mindset:** Cultivating a growth mindset involves believing that our abilities and intelligence can expand through effort and learning. Blind spot awareness plays a pivotal role in fostering a growth mindset by highlighting areas where we can develop and enhance ourselves. It motivates us to welcome challenges and perceive setbacks as chances for personal growth. Personal development is an ongoing journey, and blind spot awareness is integral to this process. Acknowledging our blind spots and actively addressing them enables continuous growth, learning, and the continual pursuit of becoming the best versions of ourselves.

Engage in Self-Reflection: A Journey of Personal Insight

Take some time to consider your own actions and thought processes. Consider asking yourself, "What are my biases?" What routines do I have that might be stifling my potential? "What sets off my bad feelings?" You can become more conscious of your blind spots by thinking back on your actions.

Self-reflection is a powerful tool for uncovering and addressing your blind spots. It involves introspection and an honest examination of your thoughts, emotions, behaviours, and patterns of action. Here are some self-reflection techniques to help you gain personal insight:

- **Journaling:** Keeping a journal allows you to record your thoughts, emotions, and experiences. Regular journaling provides a written record of your journey and enables you to track patterns, triggers, and areas for improvement.

- **Meditation**: Mindfulness meditation involves focusing on the present moment without judgment. This practice encourages self-awareness by allowing you to observe your thoughts, emotions, and bodily sensations. Meditation can help you recognise patterns and reactions that may be blind spots.

- **Self-Questioning:** Ask yourself probing questions to delve into your motivations, beliefs, and behaviours. Questions like, "Why do I react this way in certain situations?" and "What are the underlying beliefs that drive my actions?" can lead to valuable insights.

- **Feedback Analysis:** After receiving feedback from others, take time to analyse and reflect on the feedback. Consider whether the feedback aligns with your self-perception and identify areas for improvement.

- **Regular Check-Ins:** Make it a habit to periodically check in with yourself. This can involve setting aside time for self-reflection and personal assessment. It's an opportunity to assess your goals, values, and progress.

- **Retrospective Thinking:** After significant events or experiences, engage in retrospective thinking. Evaluate what went well, what didn't, and what you learned from the situation. This retrospective approach helps you uncover blind spots by reviewing past actions and their outcomes.

- **Surround Yourself with Diverse Perspectives**: Interact with people who have different perspectives and backgrounds. This exposure to diversity can challenge your assumptions and broaden your understanding of the world, revealing blind spots you may not have been aware of.

By incorporating self-reflection into your routine, you can actively work to uncover and address your blind spots. It's a continuous journey of self-discovery and personal growth.

Challenge Your Assumptions: Questioning Your Beliefs

We all have assumptions about the world around us, but if we're not careful, these assumptions could turn into blind spots. Asking yourself "Is this really true?" or "What evidence do I have to support this belief?" will force you to re-evaluate your assumptions. It is possible to become more conscious of your biases by challenging your presumptions.

Blind spots can emerge from unchecked assumptions and beliefs that go unexamined. Challenging your assumptions and beliefs is a critical step in addressing these blind spots. Here's how you can do it:

- **Question Your Beliefs:** Begin by identifying beliefs or assumptions you hold. These could be related to your abilities, values, or the way you perceive the world. For instance, you might believe that you're not good at public speaking.

- **Seek Contradictory Evidence:** Ask yourself whether there is evidence that contradicts your belief. In the public speaking example, you might recall instances where you received positive feedback on your speaking abilities.

- **Consider Alternative Perspectives:** Try to see things from a different point of view. In the public speaking case, consider the possibility that you have room for improvement, but you're not inherently bad at it.

- **Engage in Open Discussions:** Engage in open discussions with others who hold different beliefs or perspectives. This can challenge your assumptions and lead to more balanced views.

- **Embrace a Growth Mindset:** A growth mindset is the belief that abilities and intelligence can be developed through effort and learning. Embracing this mindset can help you overcome fixed beliefs that may be blind spots.

- **Regularly Reassess Your Beliefs:** Make it a habit to periodically reassess your beliefs and assumptions. As you learn and grow, your perspectives can change.

Challenging your assumptions and beliefs is a way to actively address your blind spots and expand your understanding of yourself and the world around you. It requires openness to change and a commitment to personal growth.

Develop Empathy: Understanding Others' Perspectives

A lack of empathy can be rooted in various factors, often shaping an individual's ability to connect with and understand the emotions of others. Empathy exists on a spectrum, encompassing both cognitive and emotional components. Some individuals may experience an imbalance between cognitive empathy, which involves understanding another person's perspective intellectually, and emotional empathy, which involves sharing the emotional experience of others. This distinction can result in challenges in recognising or responding to the emotional needs of those around them.

Certain personality disorders, such as narcissistic personality disorder or antisocial personality disorder, have been associated with diminished empathy. Individuals with these disorders may struggle to engage emotionally and may find it difficult to empathise with others. Experiences of significant trauma can lead to the development of defence mechanisms that distance individuals emotionally. Similarly, past negative interpersonal experiences, such as betrayal or rejection, may contribute to a reluctance to emotionally engage with others.

Cultural and environmental influences play a crucial role in shaping empathy. Upbringing and societal norms can contribute to an individual's understanding and expression of empathy. Environments lacking positive role models for empathy or encouraging self-centred behaviour may contribute to a diminished capacity for empathy.

High levels of stress or burnout can narrow an individual's focus, making it challenging to attend to the emotions of others. Chronic stress may prioritise an individual's emotional well-being over their ability to empathise with those around them. A fear of vulnerability can also play a role, causing individuals to emotionally shut down and making it difficult to connect with the emotions of others.

Empathy is the capacity to comprehend and share the emotions of others. We can become more conscious of our own prejudices and blind spots by engaging in empathy exercises. Think about how things might be and try to see things from someone else's perspective.

Empathy is a powerful tool for uncovering and addressing blind spots, particularly those related to our interactions with others. Here are some strategies to develop empathy and gain insights into your blind spots:

- **Active Listening:** When engaging with others, practice active listening. This means giving your full attention to the speaker, asking clarifying questions, and genuinely seeking to understand their perspective and emotions.

- **Put Yourself in Their Shoes:** Try to imagine yourself in the other person's position. What might they be feeling, thinking, or experiencing? This exercise helps you develop a deeper understanding of their perspective.

- **Ask Open-Ended Questions:** Encourage others to share their thoughts and feelings by asking open-ended questions. These questions invite more expansive responses and provide insights into their emotions and perspectives.

- **Read Widely:** Engage with literature and podcasts that explore diverse experiences and viewpoints. This broadens your understanding of different perspectives and can challenge your own biases and blind spots.

- **Engage in Perspective-Taking Exercises:** Deliberately engage in exercises that encourage you to view the world from someone else's perspective. This can involve role-playing or imagining scenarios from another person's viewpoint.

- **Practice Empathetic Communication:** When communicating with others, express understanding, and empathy. Acknowledge their feelings and experiences, even if you don't fully share their perspective.

    Empathy is a skill that can be developed over time through conscious effort. By actively working on your empathetic abilities, you can better understand the perspectives and experiences of others, which in turn helps you uncover and address your own blind spots related to interpersonal relationships. Incorporating these strategies into your daily life can contribute to improved self-awareness and personal growth. Uncovering and addressing blind spots is an ongoing journey, and these techniques can help you become more conscious of your biases, assumptions, and areas for improvement.

Seeking Professional Guidance: Navigating Blind Spots with a Therapist or Coach

Sometimes, recognising and addressing your blind spots may require the guidance of a professional. A therapist or coach can provide valuable insights and strategies for personal growth and self-improvement.

Therapists are trained to help individuals address emotional and psychological blind spots. They can assist you in exploring your thoughts, emotions, and behaviours and help you identify patterns that may be holding you back. Therapy is particularly beneficial for addressing deep-seated blind spots related to trauma, self-esteem, and mental health.

Coaches, on the other hand, specialise in personal and professional development. They can help you uncover blind spots related to your goals, career, and relationships. Coaches offer guidance, support, and strategies to help you address your blind spots and work toward your desired outcomes.

When seeking professional guidance to address your blind spots, consider the following:

- **Therapist or Coach Specialisation:** Look for a therapist or coach who specialises in the areas you want to address. For emotional and psychological issues, consider a therapist. For personal development and goal achievement, a coach may be more suitable.

- **Compatibility:** Choose a professional with whom you feel comfortable and can build a trusting relationship. Open and honest communication is crucial in addressing blind spots.

- **Set Clear Goals:** Define your goals and what you hope to achieve through therapy or coaching. Discuss these goals with your chosen professional to ensure alignment.

- **Regular Sessions:** Commit to regular sessions with your therapist or coach. Consistency is key in addressing blind spots and making progress.

- **Feedback and Homework:** Be open to receiving feedback and completing assigned tasks or exercises between sessions. These can help you actively work on your blind spots.

- **Monitor Progress:** Track your progress over time. Reflect on the changes and improvements you've made and discuss these with your therapist or coach.

Seeking professional guidance is a proactive step in addressing your blind spots and making positive changes in your life. Professionals can offer tailored strategies and support to help you navigate your blind spots effectively.

Farzaneh Ghadirian

Chapter 8
Nurturing Empathy in Children: The Cornerstone of Resilience and Why Some Children Struggle to Bounce Back in Challenging Times

Empathy, the ability to understand and share the feelings of another, is a fundamental aspect of human social interaction. It's a quality that plays a pivotal role in forming meaningful relationships and is inextricably linked to resilience, the capacity to bounce back from adversity. In this narrative, we will explore the profound significance of nurturing empathy in children as the cornerstone of resilience. Additionally, we will delve into the reasons why certain children find it challenging to be resilient in the face of adversity, with a particular focus on empathy as a crucial factor.

Empathy, a complex psychological concept comprising cognitive and emotional dimensions, plays a crucial role in the development of resilience, defined as the capacity to adapt positively in the face of adversity and stress. Cognitive empathy involves understanding others' perspectives, while emotional empathy entails sharing their emotional experiences.

In fostering empathy in children, it becomes essential to highlight its profound connection with resilience. Empathetic children tend to cultivate positive relationships and offer support to others. These relationships, in return, become a valuable source of social support. When children feel connected and supported, they gain the tools needed to navigate challenging situations and setbacks. This network of social support significantly enhances their resilience, allowing them to draw strength from these relationships during difficult times. Moreover, empathy fosters emotional regulation. By understanding and recognising the emotions of others, children learn to manage their own emotions more effectively. When faced with adversity, emotionally regulated children are better equipped to cope with stress, anxiety, and other negative emotions. This ability to self-regulate contributes significantly to their resilience in challenging situations.

Empathetic children also tend to possess better problem-solving skills. They are more likely to approach challenges with a solution-focused mindset, seeking ways to alleviate the suffering of others and themselves. Problem-solving is a crucial aspect of resilience, as it enables individuals to find constructive ways to overcome adversity. Furthermore, empathy promotes perspective-taking. The ability to take another person's perspective is a key component of cognitive empathy. Children who can understand different points of view are more likely to adapt and adjust their thinking when confronted with adversity. This adaptive thinking is a central aspect of resilience, allowing children to reframe their experiences and identify opportunities for growth even in difficult situations.

While nurturing empathy in children is pivotal for resilience, numerous factors can hinder its development, impacting a child's ability to bounce back in the face of adversity. Recognising these barriers is essential for effectively addressing them. Supportive relationships are the foundation of resilience. Children who lack these connections may find it challenging to develop resilience because they lack the essential safety net of emotional support. Such relationships provide children with a sense of value, love, and understanding, which is crucial for their ability to confront challenges.

Traumatic events such as abuse, neglect, or exposure to violence can lead to deep emotional scars, making it difficult for children to rebound from challenging situations. The development of conditions like anxiety, depression, and post-traumatic stress can further hinder their resilience. Effective coping strategies are vital for resilience, and children who have not been exposed to or taught these mechanisms may struggle when confronted with adversity. In such cases, they may resort to maladaptive behaviours, which can exacerbate their challenges in bouncing back from adversity. Self-esteem, the perception of one's self-worth, is a foundational component of resilience. Children with low self-esteem may doubt their abilities to overcome challenges, leading to a lack of self-efficacy. This self-doubt can make it difficult for them to bounce back from distressing events.

Effective emotional regulation is a fundamental aspect of resilience. Children who struggle with emotional regulation may find it challenging to rebound from adversity, as they may experience intense and overwhelming emotional reactions. Social connections and social skills are essential for resilience. Children who experience social isolation may have limited access to the social support networks that are crucial for coping with adversity. Loneliness and social isolation can exacerbate feelings of helplessness, further impeding their resilience. Cultural and societal norms and expectations significantly influence how children perceive and respond to adversity. Different cultures have varying attitudes towards resilience, with some emphasising its importance and others promoting passivity or reliance on external factors. Societal factors like discrimination can create substantial barriers to resilience, as children may face unique challenges not experienced by others. Children with learning disabilities or certain neurological conditions, such as autism, can also encounter distinct challenges in the development of resilience. These conditions may affect a child's capacity to adapt to and learn from adverse experiences, necessitating tailored support and interventions to help them build resilience.

Growing up in an economically disadvantaged environment can significantly hinder resilience. Chronic stress and the uncertainty associated with financial instability can lead children to focus primarily on survival, leaving limited room for the cultivation of resilience. In such circumstances, immediate needs take precedence, making it difficult for children to focus on resilience-building.

High parental or societal expectations can create a fear of failure in children. This fear can hinder their ability to bounce back from setbacks, as the pressure to meet unrealistic standards may lead to a paralysing fear of disappointing others or themselves. Perfectionist tendencies can make children overly risk-averse, preventing them from engaging in activities where they might potentially fail, and, as a result, stunting the development of their resilience.

Children with chronic physical or mental health issues face significant barriers to resilience. These challenges often consume a child's physical and emotional resources, leaving them with limited capacity to deal with additional stressors. While well-intentioned, overprotective parenting can hinder the development of resilience. Children who are excessively shielded from adversity may struggle when faced with challenges on their own, as they may become overly dependent on others to solve problems.

However, despite the importance of empathy in fostering resilience, there are various barriers that some children face in developing this vital trait. These barriers can range from the absence of supportive relationships to traumatic experiences, limited coping skills, low self-esteem, inadequate emotional regulation, social isolation, cultural and societal factors, learning disabilities, financial instability, unrealistic expectations, perfectionism, health issues, and overprotective parenting.

Recognising these barriers is the first step in addressing them effectively. Providing children with the necessary support, resources, and guidance is essential to help them overcome these obstacles and build resilience. By fostering supportive relationships, teaching coping skills, addressing trauma, promoting emotional regulation, and creating environments that encourage self-esteem and problem-solving, we can empower children to develop the resilience they need to thrive in the face of adversity. Empathy remains the cornerstone, but it's only one part of the complex journey toward resilience, a journey that requires the collective efforts of parents, caregivers, educators, and society.

Chapter 9
The Delicate Art of Vulnerability in Parenting: Nurturing Healthy Behaviour in Our Children While Avoiding Oversharing

In the intricate and often challenging art of parenting, one aspect often overlooked is the importance of vulnerability. It's not just about being strong and infallible; it's about showing our authentic selves to our children. In this discussion, we will explore the profound significance of vulnerability in parenting, how it can model healthy behaviour for our children, and the transformative impact it can have on family dynamics.

Vulnerability, at its core, is the willingness to expose our true selves, including our emotions, fears, and imperfections. It's the act of letting our guard down and allowing our children to see the raw and unfiltered version of us, warts and all. Embracing vulnerability is a testament to the authenticity and a commitment to forging deeper connections within our families.

When parents display vulnerability, they teach their children to understand, manage, and express their emotions. This emotional intelligence equips children with the tools to navigate the complex landscape of feelings and relationships. Vulnerability not only allows children to see their parents as multidimensional beings but also enables them to relate to their parents' emotions and experiences. This, in turn, cultivates empathy, as children begin to recognise and understand the feelings and struggles of others.

When parents show vulnerability, they create a safe environment for their children to be themselves without fear of judgment. This nurturing atmosphere encourages open communication and strengthens the parent-child bond.

Children who witness their parents' vulnerability learn that it's okay to make mistakes and face challenges. They understand that vulnerability isn't a sign of weakness but a demonstration of courage. This understanding enhances their resilience, enabling them to bounce back from adversity with grace. When parents model vulnerability, they encourage authenticity in their children. In an era where societal pressures often lead to pretence, the ability to be one's genuine self is a precious gift that parents can bestow upon their children.

The power of vulnerability is a force that transcends weakness and reveals the remarkable strength of the human spirit. In a world that often values stoicism and masks, embracing vulnerability is a transformative act that has the potential to touch lives in profound ways. It is through vulnerability that we connect, learn, and grow, and its impact on our personal development, relationships, and overall well-being cannot be overstated.

Vulnerability is the gateway to authentic human connections. When we allow ourselves to be vulnerable, we open our hearts to others, inviting them to share in our joys, sorrows, and fears. This openness creates trust and deepens the bonds we form with our loved ones. Vulnerability is the key to understanding and empathy, as it enables us to recognise the common thread of human experience that binds us all.

Moreover, vulnerability has the remarkable power to enhance resilience. It is in our moments of vulnerability that we discover the strength to confront adversity head-on. When we acknowledge our imperfections and fears, we become better equipped to face life's challenges with grace and courage. This self-awareness and acceptance of our vulnerabilities are the building blocks of emotional resilience, enabling us to bounce back from setbacks with a renewed sense of purpose.

In families, the power of vulnerability can transform dynamics and relationships. When parents model vulnerability for their children, they not only teach them valuable life lessons but also create an atmosphere of trust and openness within the family unit. Children who witness their parents embracing vulnerability understand that it is a sign of courage and authenticity, and this understanding shapes them into empathetic, resilient, and authentic individuals.

Understanding Vulnerability in Parenting

Vulnerability, in the context of parenting, is often misunderstood or overlooked. It doesn't mean burdening children with our deepest fears and insecurities, but rather it involves allowing them to see us as human beings with our own emotions and vulnerabilities. Vulnerability doesn't imply oversharing or overwhelming children with age-inappropriate details. Instead, it's a thoughtful sharing of appropriate aspects of our emotional experiences. This sharing can include acknowledging when we make mistakes, expressing our feelings, and demonstrating healthy ways to cope with challenges.

Emotional Intelligence and Empathy

One of the primary benefits of modelling vulnerability in parenting is the development of emotional intelligence and empathy in children. When parents share their emotions and experiences, it provides children with a window into the complexities of human feelings. Children learn that it's okay to feel sad, angry, anxious, or even unsure at times, and they begin to understand that these emotions are part of the human experience.

Furthermore, when parents express vulnerability by sharing their own emotional challenges, it allows children to relate to those experiences. They realise that their parents have felt the same way, which can be especially comforting during moments of personal struggle. This, in turn, fosters empathy, as children become more attuned to the emotions and experiences of others, both within and outside the family.

Building Trust and Open Communication

Vulnerability is a powerful tool in building trust within the family. When children see that their parents are honest about their feelings and experiences, they feel secure and valued. This sense of security promotes open communication, as children learn that they can confide in their parents without fear of judgment.

In a family where vulnerability is encouraged, discussions about challenging topics, such as bullying, peer pressure, or personal difficulties, become more accessible. Children are more likely to seek guidance and share their concerns with parents who have demonstrated that it's safe to be open about their feelings.

Moreover, when parents openly discuss their own mistakes and challenges, it normalises the idea that no one is perfect. This can relieve the pressure on children to be flawless and instead encourages them to learn from their missteps.

Fostering Resilience

Another essential aspect of parenting is fostering resilience in children. Resilience is the ability to bounce back from adversity, and vulnerability plays a pivotal role in this process. When parents model vulnerability, they demonstrate that facing challenges and making mistakes is a part of life. This understanding equips children with the mindset and skills to confront adversity with courage.

Parents can share stories of their own setbacks and how they overcame them. These personal narratives serve as powerful examples of resilience in action. When children witness their parents' journeys of perseverance, it inspires them to adopt a similar attitude when confronted with difficulties.

Additionally, parents can teach their children problem-solving skills and the importance of seeking help when needed. By showing vulnerability in their willingness to ask for assistance or advice, parents impart the value of collaboration and learning from others.

Encouraging Authenticity

In today's world, there is often immense pressure on individuals to conform to societal expectations and norms. Children, in particular, can feel the weight of these expectations. By modelling vulnerability, parents encourage authenticity in their children. When children see their parents being true to themselves, flaws and all, it sends a powerful message. It communicates that they don't need to pretend to be someone they're not. Instead, they can embrace their true selves, with all their imperfections and unique qualities. Furthermore, by witnessing their parents' vulnerability, children understand that it's okay to express their individuality and pursue their passions, even if they differ from the expectations of others. This self-acceptance is a precious gift that parents can bestow upon their children, fostering a sense of confidence and self-worth.

Balancing Vulnerability in Parenting: Protecting Children from Emotional Oversharing

The delicate balance of embracing vulnerability in parenting extends to the cautious approach of not oversharing with children. Oversharing can have negative consequences on the emotional well-being and development of children, and thus, it's vital to consider the child's age, emotional maturity, and readiness to process certain information.

Children are inherently sensitive to their parent's emotions and are deeply influenced by their behaviours and attitudes. However, there is a fine line between fostering open communication and overwhelming them with adult complexities.

- **Emotional Burden:** While children possess a natural inclination for empathy, they lack the emotional maturity to navigate the full weight of their parents' emotional struggles. When parents overshare their difficulties, it places an undue burden on children, exposing them to emotional challenges beyond their capacity to comprehend. This can evoke a range of psychological impacts on children.

Children, being impressionable and often perceiving their parents as emotional anchors, may internalise the shared struggles as their own. This internalisation can lead to a distorted sense of responsibility for their parents' emotional well-being. They might erroneously believe that they are somehow accountable for resolving or alleviating their parents' distress. This misplaced responsibility can create a profound sense of anxiety and stress in children. The psychological impact extends further as children may experience a blurring of boundaries between their own emotions and those of their parents. This lack of emotional delineation can hinder the development of a healthy emotional identity, making it challenging for children to differentiate their feelings from the emotional states of their parents.

Moreover, consistent exposure to parental emotional struggles can contribute to an environment of heightened tension and unpredictability for children. The emotional atmosphere at home becomes charged with unresolved issues and distress, potentially leading to a sense of insecurity and unease. This emotional turmoil can manifest in various ways, including disruptions in children's mood, behaviour, and overall emotional well-being.

- **Confusion:** Oversharing complex adult issues with children, who lack the emotional maturity and life experience to fully grasp such intricacies, can have profound psychological implications. This act of oversharing may lead to a state of confusion, leaving children disoriented and anxious, ultimately impeding their emotional development.

Children, in their formative years, are still in the process of developing cognitive and emotional frameworks to understand the world around them. When confronted with adult issues beyond their comprehension, they may struggle to make sense of the complexities involved. This cognitive dissonance can result in a state of confusion, where the child grapples with conflicting emotions and thoughts, hindering their ability to form a coherent understanding of the shared information.

The confusion induced by oversharing can manifest in heightened levels of anxiety for children. The inability to fully comprehend adult issues creates a sense of uncertainty and unpredictability in their emotional environment. This heightened anxiety may interfere with the child's day-to-day functioning, impacting their mood, behaviour, and overall emotional well-being.

Furthermore, confusion stemming from oversharing can disrupt the natural progression of a child's emotional development. Rather than navigating age-appropriate emotional challenges, children may find themselves thrust into the complexities of adult issues prematurely. This disruption in the natural developmental trajectory can impede the acquisition of essential emotional coping skills and resilience.

- **Loss of Trust:** Oversharing, particularly when it involves divulging inappropriate or overwhelming information, can precipitate a loss of trust between parents and children. The psychological implications of this loss of trust reverberate through the parent-child relationship, impacting the child's willingness to confide in their parents and the overall dynamics of trust-building. Children inherently rely on their parents as sources of guidance, support, and emotional security. When parents overshare, especially when sharing information that is beyond the child's developmental capacity or is deemed inappropriate, it disrupts the established dynamic of trust. The child may perceive the parent as a source of confusion or discomfort rather than a reliable figure for emotional support.

The psychological impact of this loss of trust is multifaceted. Firstly, it can lead to emotional distancing between the child and the parent. The child, now wary of potential oversharing, may become guarded in their interactions with the parent. This guardedness serves as a protective mechanism to shield themselves from exposure to information that may cause confusion or distress. Secondly, the loss of trust can hinder open communication within the parent-child relationship. A child who has experienced oversharing may be less likely to share their thoughts, feelings, or challenges with the parent. The fear of being exposed to inappropriate information may lead the child to withdraw emotionally, creating a communication barrier between parent and child.

Additionally, the loss of trust can impact the child's overall sense of security and attachment. Trust is fundamental in building secure attachments, and when this trust is compromised, the child may struggle to form healthy emotional connections. This can influence the child's future relationships, as the learned behaviour of guardedness and reluctance to confide may persist into adulthood.

- Role Reversal: Oversharing can induce a role reversal dynamic, compelling children to take on the unexpected responsibility of providing emotional support to their parents. This reversal disrupts the conventional parent-child dynamic and has significant psychological implications, fostering feelings of insecurity, and instability, and impacting the child's overall emotional well-being.

Children inherently look to their parents for emotional guidance, support, and a sense of security. When parents overshare their emotional struggles, placing the burden on the child to provide support, it upends the established roles within the family structure. This sudden shift can be disorienting and challenging for the child, who may grapple with the newfound responsibility of caretaking for their parent's emotional needs.

The psychological implications of role reversal due to oversharing are profound. Firstly, it can create a sense of emotional insecurity in the child. The child may feel uncertain about their own emotional needs being met, as the traditional source of support, their parent, is now relying on them for support. This emotional insecurity can manifest as anxiety, stress, or a sense of overwhelm in the child. Secondly, role reversal disrupts the child's development of a healthy sense of self. Instead of focusing on their own emotional growth and exploration, the child is prematurely thrust into the role of caregiver. This premature caregiving responsibility may hinder the child's ability to establish a strong sense of identity and self-esteem, as their emotional energy is directed outward rather than inward.

The instability caused by role reversal can impact the child's overall emotional well-being. Children thrive in environments where roles and expectations are clear and consistent. Oversharing disrupts this stability, introducing an element of unpredictability and blurring the boundaries between parent and child roles. The child may struggle to navigate their own emotional landscape while simultaneously shouldering the emotional needs of their parents.

- **Loss of Childhood:** Oversharing can accelerate the loss of childhood innocence, thrusting children into the complex realm of adult issues prematurely. This untimely exposure deprives them of the freedom to grow and develop at their own pace. Childhood, traditionally a time for exploration, learning, and emotional growth, becomes overshadowed by the weight of adult concerns, with profound psychological impacts that may extend into adulthood.

The psychological implications of the loss of childhood due to oversharing are multifaceted and can manifest in various aspects of an individual's adult life.

Firstly, there may be challenges in establishing a healthy sense of boundaries. Childhood is a crucial period for developing an understanding of personal boundaries, both in terms of physical and emotional limits. Oversharing disrupts this natural process by blurring the lines between parent and child roles, potentially leading to difficulties in recognising and asserting personal boundaries in adulthood.

Secondly, premature exposure to adult issues can impact the child's ability to form and maintain healthy relationships in adulthood. The child may struggle to relate to peers who had a more typical childhood experience, potentially feeling isolated or lacking common ground. Additionally, the emotional burden placed on the child may lead to challenges in establishing boundaries within future relationships, as the learned pattern of caretaking for others' emotional needs may persist.

Furthermore, the loss of childhood innocence may contribute to a sense of emotional dysregulation in adulthood. Childhood is a time for developing emotional resilience and coping mechanisms. When this period is disrupted by exposure to adult concerns, the child may not have the opportunity to develop these essential emotional skills fully. As a result, they may face challenges in managing stress, anxiety, and other emotions in adulthood.

The loss of childhood innocence can also impact the individual's overall well-being and mental health. Childhood experiences shape the foundation of one's psychological resilience and coping strategies. Oversharing disrupts this foundational development, potentially contributing to difficulties in navigating life's challenges, coping with adversity, and maintaining emotional well-being in adulthood.

The intricate correlation between invasion of privacy, specifically through oversharing, and the formation of personal identity is a nuanced psychological phenomenon. Privacy serves as a critical component in the complex process of identity development, particularly during the formative years of childhood. In this developmental phase, children require a secure and private mental space where they can freely explore their thoughts, emotions, and values, thus facilitating the cultivation of a distinct sense of self. Oversharing disrupts the natural exploration of a child's private mental space by encroaching upon its sanctity. When children are exposed to their parents' struggles, this external influence can potentially lead to identity confusion or the assimilation of external challenges into the child's emerging sense of self. This interference poses the risk of significantly impacting their ability to navigate personal growth and self-discovery in adulthood. The exposure to external struggles, such as those faced by parents, may result in the child internalising these challenges as part of their own identity. This assimilation can blur the boundaries between the child's authentic self and the external struggles to which they have been exposed, potentially influencing their beliefs, values, and emotional responses. Furthermore, the constant exposure to external influences, particularly those beyond the child's control, may create a sense of vulnerability and uncertainty about their own thoughts and feelings. This intrusion could potentially limit the child's ability to develop a strong and resilient sense of self, hindering their capacity to navigate the complexities of personal growth and self-discovery during adulthood.

Finding the right balance between embracing vulnerability and safeguarding children's emotions requires a conscious approach. Parents need to consider their child's age, emotional maturity, and individual temperament when diving into conversations about vulnerability. While it's crucial to encourage openness, authenticity, and support, it's equally important to be mindful of what's age-appropriate and respectful of the child's boundaries.
Open communication is the key to this delicate dance. Parents can talk to their children, letting them know it's okay to share feelings and concerns. But here's the catch—some topics might be better discussed with other adults or professionals. Striking this balance ensures that children feel free to express themselves in an environment that's safe, where they're truly heard, and where love abounds. The goal is to create a space where children feel secure without being burdened by the weight of adult issues.

Farzaneh Ghadirian

Chapter 10
The Power of Positive Reinforcement: Fostering Virtuous Behaviour in Our Children While Avoiding the Pitfalls of Negative Reinforcement

Parenting is often described as one of the most challenging and rewarding experiences in life. As parents, we play a pivotal role in shaping our children's character and behaviour. In an increasingly complex and fast-paced world, instilling virtues and good behaviour in our children has become more critical than ever. Positive reinforcement, a psychological principle that involves rewarding desired behaviours, has emerged as a powerful tool for nurturing virtuous behaviour in children.

Understanding Positive Reinforcement

Positive reinforcement is a fundamental concept in psychology and behavioural science. It involves the use of rewards or favourable consequences to encourage and strengthen desired behaviours. The key components of positive reinforcement include identifying the target behaviour, delivering a reward immediately after the behaviour, and ensuring that the reward is something that the individual values. Positive reinforcement works on the principle that individuals are more likely to repeat behaviours that lead to positive outcomes. In the context of child development, positive reinforcement can be a powerful tool for encouraging virtuous behaviour. Virtues such as kindness, empathy, honesty, responsibility, and respect are qualities that parents often seek to instil in their children. Using positive reinforcement, parents can help their children develop these virtues by reinforcing behaviours that exemplify them.

The Importance of Virtuous Behaviour in Children

Before delving into the application of positive reinforcement, it's essential to understand why nurturing virtuous behaviour in children is so crucial. Virtues are the building blocks of a well-rounded, responsible, and compassionate individual. They not only lead to better interpersonal relationships but also contribute to a more harmonious and just society. Here are some of the key reasons why virtuous behaviour is essential in children:

- **Building Strong Character:** Developing robust character in children is intricately tied to the cultivation of virtues, which serve as the bedrock of their moral and emotional foundation. Delving into the psychological aspects of this process unveils a profound connection between virtue development and the intricate workings of a child's psyche.

  At the heart of strong character lies the cultivation of virtues such as honesty, integrity, and kindness. From a psychological standpoint, these virtues are not merely abstract concepts but powerful influencers that shape a child's cognitive and emotional landscape. The manifestation of virtues is often intertwined with the development of a child's sense of self and their understanding of the social world.

  Honesty, as a virtue, plays a pivotal role in a child's psychological development. When children are encouraged to be honest, they navigate the delicate balance between truthfulness and the fear of repercussions. The practice of honesty fosters a sense of integrity, where the child learns to align their actions with their internal moral compass. This alignment contributes significantly to the formation of a stable and cohesive sense of self.

Integrity, as a virtue, extends beyond mere adherence to ethical principles. Psychologically, it involves the integration of various aspects of a child's personality and values. Children with a strong sense of integrity showcase coherence in their thoughts, emotions, and actions. This internal harmony is a testament to the robust character that is being nurtured.

Kindness, as a virtue, becomes a psychological anchor for children's social and emotional well-being. Acts of kindness, whether receiving or extending, create positive emotional experiences. These experiences contribute to the development of empathy, compassion, and a sense of interconnectedness with others. As children engage in kind acts, they forge connections that reinforce a positive view of themselves within the social fabric.

The interplay of virtues in character development extends beyond isolated behaviours. It involves the integration of cognitive processes such as moral reasoning and emotional regulation. Children who internalise virtues engage in complex cognitive processes where they assess situations, empathise with others, and make decisions aligned with their moral values. These cognitive processes, intertwined with emotional experiences, lay the foundation for a strong character.

- **Healthy Relationships:** Fostering virtues in children lays the groundwork for the development of healthy relationships, a process intricately intertwined with various aspects that shape their social interactions and emotional intelligence.

Virtuous children, characterised by qualities like empathy, understanding, and conflict resolution skills, exhibit resilience that significantly influences their relationship dynamics. The cultivation of empathy, for instance, is a cornerstone for positive social interactions. When children develop the capacity to understand and share the feelings of others, it enhances their emotional intelligence. This heightened emotional awareness becomes an asset, enabling them to navigate the intricacies of social relationships with greater sensitivity.

Understanding, as a virtue, extends beyond mere cognitive comprehension. It involves the capacity to grasp the nuanced emotions and perspectives of others. Children who embody this virtue engage in complex cognitive processes, such as perspective-taking, which contribute to their ability to connect with peers and adults on a deeper emotional level. This depth of understanding facilitates the building of meaningful and authentic relationships.

The virtue of conflict resolution plays a pivotal role in shaping the approach children adopt when faced with interpersonal challenges. Children equipped with effective conflict resolution skills develop a sense of self-efficacy in managing social tensions. This self-efficacy is rooted in the belief that they can navigate conflicts successfully, contributing to a positive self-concept and bolstering their overall emotional well-being.

Moreover, the psychological benefits of virtuous behaviour extend to the social environment. Virtuous children contribute to the creation of a positive and harmonious social atmosphere. Their empathetic and understanding nature fosters a sense of trust and cooperation among peers, creating a psychologically safe space for interpersonal connections to flourish. The development of virtuous qualities in children is not a passive process; it involves active engagement with cognitive and emotional dimensions. As children internalise virtues like empathy, understanding, and conflict resolution, they engage in ongoing processes that shape their social behaviours. These processes include perspective-taking, emotional regulation, and problem-solving skills, all of which contribute to the establishment of healthy relationship dynamics.

- **Success in Life:** The cultivation of virtues in individuals sets the stage for multifaceted success, encompassing both personal and professional realms, with profound consciousness underpinnings shaping their journey.

    Virtuous individuals exhibit resilience that becomes a catalyst for success in diverse life domains. One key virtue contributing to this success is integrity. Integrity forms the bedrock of a cohesive and authentic self-concept. When individuals consistently align their actions with their values, they experience a sense of internal harmony and authenticity. This coherence enhances their self-esteem and self-efficacy, empowering them to pursue and achieve personal goals with a steadfast mindset.

    Furthermore, virtues like perseverance and resilience play pivotal roles in the landscape of success. The ability to persevere through challenges is closely tied to constructs such as grit and mental toughness. Virtuous individuals, equipped with these qualities, display a tenacity that enables them to navigate setbacks with a growth-oriented mindset. This resilience fosters an adaptive response to adversity, contributing to increased motivation and the pursuit of long-term goals.

    The virtue of kindness, often overlooked in discussions of success, holds significant implications. Acts of kindness trigger the release of oxytocin, a neurochemical associated with bonding and positive social interactions. Virtuous individuals, by engaging in compassionate and altruistic behaviours, experience a psychological boost in mood and overall well-being. This positive psychological state, in turn, creates a conducive internal environment for pursuing and attaining personal and professional success.

    Trust, a foundational element of virtuous individuals' success, operates as a currency in interpersonal relationships. The establishment of trust involves a complex interplay of factors such as reliability, honesty, and empathy. Virtuous individuals, recognised for their integrity and ethical conduct, naturally evoke trust from others. Trust forms the basis for successful collaborations, effective communication, and the building of enduring social connections, all of which contribute to success in personal and professional spheres.

- **Contributing to Society:** The impact of virtuous behaviour extends far beyond individual relationships, resonating deeply within the fabric of society. Virtuous individuals, guided by values such as kindness, empathy, and a sense of responsibility, play a pivotal role in fostering a communal environment characterised by cooperation, compassion, and social cohesion. At its core, the virtue of kindness is a catalyst for prosocial behaviour and community well-being. Engaging in acts of kindness triggers a positive feedback loop. The individuals who exhibit kindness experience an elevation in mood, an increase in oxytocin levels—the "love hormone" associated with social bonding—and a sense of fulfilment. This positive state not only enhances the well-being of virtuous individuals but also radiates outward, influencing the overall emotional climate of the community.

  Volunteerism and community service, often integral components of virtuous behaviour, contribute to the betterment of society on a broader scale. The act of volunteering is associated with a sense of purpose and fulfilment. Virtuous individuals find intrinsic motivation in contributing to the welfare of others and the community at large. This motivation stems from satisfaction derived from making a positive impact, reinforcing a sense of social connectedness, and fostering a collective responsibility for the well-being of society.

  Moreover, the benefits of virtuous behaviour in contributing to society are not confined to the individual performers alone. Acts of kindness and community service create a ripple effect, influencing others to partake in similar benevolent actions. This social contagion of virtue is grounded in phenomena such as social learning and normative influence. When virtuous behaviour is observed and reinforced within a community, it becomes a shared value, shaping the collective psyche and encouraging a culture of altruism and communal support.

- **Emotional Well-Being:** The cultivation of virtues plays a profound role in enhancing emotional well-being, fostering a positive environment that contributes to reduced stress and increased happiness. Three virtues—kindness, gratitude, and forgiveness—stand out in their impact on emotional flourishing.

    The impact of forgiveness is particularly profound in the realm of emotional well-being. Forgiveness involves releasing resentment and negative emotions toward those who have caused harm. The act of forgiveness is a transformative process that can lead to a profound sense of liberation. Instead of being trapped in a cycle of anger or hurt, individuals who practice forgiveness experience a shift in their emotional state. This shift is associated with reduced levels of stress, anxiety, and depression. Forgiveness also intersects with positive psychology, where it is recognised as a pathway to emotional freedom and increased life satisfaction. The act of forgiving is not about condoning harmful behaviour but rather about releasing the emotional burden carried by the forgiver. This process has been linked to increased well-being, improved relationships, and a greater sense of inner peace.

Now that we understand the significance of virtuous behaviour in children, let's explore the potential pitfalls of negative reinforcement.

While positive reinforcement is a valuable tool in nurturing virtuous behaviour, it's crucial to highlight the potential pitfalls of negative reinforcement and punishment. Negative reinforcement, which involves removing an unpleasant consequence to increase desired behaviour, and punishment, which involves introducing an unpleasant consequence to decrease unwanted behaviour, can have adverse effects on a child's moral development if not used judiciously.

- **Fear and Compliance:** Negative reinforcement and punishment have the potential to elicit fear and compliance rather than fostering a genuine understanding of moral principles. In instances where children are motivated to behave well solely to evade punishment, there's a risk that they may not internalise the underlying reasons behind their actions.

  Negative reinforcement involves removing an unpleasant consequence to encourage desired behaviour, while punishment introduces an unpleasant consequence to discourage unwanted behaviour, these methods can yield immediate behavioural changes, but relying solely on them may not promote a deep comprehension of moral values.

  When children associate their conduct primarily with avoiding punishment, the emphasis shifts away from internalising the intrinsic worth of virtuous behaviour. Instead, the focus becomes external, centred on steering clear of negative consequences. This external motivation may not contribute to the development of a robust moral compass or a genuine appreciation for ethical conduct. The use of fear-based tactics in discipline can create an environment where compliance is driven by anxiety rather than a heartfelt understanding of right and wrong. Children may become adept at navigating situations to escape punishment, but this proficiency may not translate into a sincere commitment to virtuous principles.

- **Resentment and Rebellion:** Excessive reliance on negative reinforcement and punishment in child discipline can give rise to feelings of resentment and rebellion. Children subjected to frequent punitive measures may develop a sense of aversion towards authority figures and harbour a negative attitude towards virtuous behaviour. When negative reinforcement and punishment are consistently applied without a balanced and understanding approach, children may perceive authority figures as oppressive or unjust. This perception can contribute to the erosion of trust and a strained relationship between children and those in positions of authority, such as parents, teachers, or caregivers.

Resentment may manifest as defiance or rebellion, with children rebelling against rules and expectations as a form of resistance. Instead of fostering an internalised understanding of virtuous conduct, the continuous use of punitive measures may lead children to associate moral behaviour with unpleasant consequences, reinforcing a negative perspective.

Negative attitudes towards virtuous behaviour may extend beyond the immediate disciplinary context. Children may carry these negative perceptions into various aspects of their lives, impacting their interactions with peers, educators, and the broader community.

- **Short-Term Solutions:** Negative reinforcement and punishment strategies typically produce short-term results. In situations where the threat of punishment is present, children may modify their behaviour temporarily to avoid the unpleasant consequences. However, once the immediate threat is lifted, there's a risk that children may revert to their previous undesirable behaviour. The effectiveness of negative reinforcement and punishment in maintaining long-term behavioural changes is limited. While these approaches can serve as deterrents at the moment, they may not instil a lasting understanding of the underlying virtues or moral principles.

- **Emotional Impact:** Negative reinforcement and punishment can have profound emotional consequences on children, influencing their mental and emotional well-being. From a psychological perspective, these approaches may lead to heightened stress, anxiety, and a diminished sense of self-worth. When a child experiences negative reinforcement, where a pleasant stimulus is removed to encourage desirable behaviour, or punishment, involving the introduction of an unpleasant consequence to deter unwanted behaviour, it can create a stressful environment. The anticipation of potential punishment or the removal of something positive can trigger the release of stress hormones, such as cortisol, in the child's body. This heightened stress response can negatively impact the child's emotional state, contributing to feelings of anxiety and apprehension. The fear of punishment may overshadow the child's ability to focus on understanding the moral or ethical principles associated with their behaviour, hindering the development of a genuine internalisation of virtues.

The use of punishment can lead to a diminished sense of self-worth. Children may internalise negative messages about themselves when subjected to punitive measures. They might perceive themselves as inherently flawed or undeserving, fostering a negative self-image. This can have long-term implications for their self-esteem and emotional resilience.

Negative reinforcement and punishment, when overused or applied without careful consideration, can create an emotionally charged environment that interferes with a child's psychological well-being, potentially impeding the development of a healthy, positive self-concept.

In our quest to raise virtuous children who not only exhibit good behaviour but also understand the underlying principles of morality, positive reinforcement emerges as a powerful and effective psychological tool. By using rewards and favourable consequences to encourage virtuous behaviours, parents can help children develop a strong moral foundation. Virtuous behaviour, including kindness, honesty, empathy, responsibility, and respect, is essential not only for individual character development but also for building a more harmonious and just society.

As parents navigate the complexities of child-rearing, it is vital to be cautious about the potential pitfalls of negative reinforcement and punishment, which can lead to fear, compliance, and short-term solutions. Instead, we should focus on nurturing virtues through positive reinforcement, open communication, and age-appropriate strategies tailored to each child's unique needs and personality.

Farzaneh Ghadirian

Chapter 11
The Dangers of Shame-Based Parenting:
Breaking the Cycle of Negative Behaviour

Shame-based parenting is a parenting style characterised by the use of shame as a primary tool for disciplining and correcting a child's behaviour. parents rely on making their children feel guilty or embarrassed about their actions to curb undesirable behaviour. Unlike discipline methods that focus on teaching and guiding, shame-based parenting centres on inducing feelings of shame, inadequacy, or unworthiness in the child.

Common tactics in shame-based parenting include harsh criticism, public embarrassment, or withholding affection as a means of punishment. The underlying belief is often that by making a child feel ashamed of their actions, they will be more likely to conform to societal or familial expectations.

Many parents who employ shame-based parenting may not consciously recognise their approach as such, as it often stems from ingrained beliefs and patterns. One significant factor contributing to this parenting style is the influence of cultural and familial upbringing. Parents may inadvertently replicate disciplinary methods they experienced in their own childhoods, normalising shame-based tactics as a means of correction. Another contributing factor is the lack of access to parenting education and resources. Without guidance on positive discipline strategies, some parents resort to methods they believe will swiftly correct their child's behaviour, even if these methods involve inducing shame.

Parenting, undoubtedly, comes with its challenges, and stress and overwhelm can lead to reactive behaviours. In moments of frustration or exhaustion, parents may opt for shame-based tactics as a seemingly quick way to gain compliance. Unrealistic expectations of children can also drive parents towards shame-based parenting. Feeling the pressure to meet certain standards, parents may resort to shame to express disappointment or frustration when their children fall short.

Cultural norms around obedience play a pivotal role, especially in societies that strongly emphasise compliance. Influenced by societal expectations, parents might turn to shame to mould their children into socially acceptable behaviours. The awareness of employing shame-based parenting is not universal among parents. Often, these patterns are deeply ingrained, and parents may not fully grasp the potential harm they are causing. Recognising one's parenting style requires self-reflection, openness to alternative approaches, and a willingness to break cycles from past generations.

The roots of shame-based parenting can be traced back to an authoritarian upbringing, where strict rules enforced through shame may have been the norm. A fear of losing control over a child's behaviour can also drive parents towards shame-based tactics as a way to regain a perceived sense of control. Parents grappling with difficulties in regulating their own emotions may encounter significant challenges when it comes to responding calmly to their children's behaviour. Emotional regulation is a crucial aspect of effective parenting, as it involves managing one's own emotions to respond appropriately to a child's actions. When parents struggle in this area, it can create a ripple effect, contributing to the adoption of shame-based parenting as a reactive response.

Emotional regulation encompasses the ability to identify, understand, and manage one's own emotions. Parents who find it challenging to regulate their emotions may experience heightened stress levels, frustration, or even anger when faced with challenging behaviour from their children. In these moments, the immediate reaction might be to assert control through shame-based tactics. The connection between parental emotional regulation and shame-based parenting lies in the reactionary nature of these responses. When parents are unable to navigate their own emotional landscape effectively, they may resort to shame as a way to regain a semblance of control or authority. It becomes a reactive strategy rather than a thoughtful, intentional approach to discipline. For example, a parent struggling with heightened emotions in response to a child's misbehaviour may react impulsively by using shame as a tool for correction. This could involve making the child feel guilty or embarrassed about their actions, with the aim of stopping the undesirable behaviour in the short term. However, this reactive use of shame fails to address the root causes of the child's behaviour or provide constructive guidance. Instead, it perpetuates a cycle where shame becomes the default response to challenging situations. Over time, children internalise this shame, impacting their self-esteem and shaping their understanding of themselves and their actions.

Shame-based parenting exerts profound and enduring effects on a child's emotional and psychological well-being. The constant exposure to shame, where a child is made to feel inadequate or unworthy in response to their behaviours, can result in a range of harmful consequences. One of the most significant impacts is the erosion of a child's self-esteem. The fear of making mistakes or falling short of expectations creates persistent anxiety, impacting both mental and physical health. Moreover, shame-based parenting can diminish a child's motivation and self-efficacy. Instead of fostering autonomy and confidence in their abilities, it instils a belief that they are inherently flawed, hindering their willingness to take on challenges and pursue personal goals and portraying a negative self-image that persists into adulthood.
This internal narrative, often established through shame-based parenting, can extend into adulthood and manifest as a phenomenon commonly known as impostor syndrome.

Impostor syndrome is a psychological pattern where individuals, despite external evidence of their competence and accomplishments, persistently doubt their abilities and fear being exposed as frauds. The roots of impostor syndrome can be intricately connected to the negative self-image cultivated by the consistent experience of shame during childhood. When children are made to feel fundamentally flawed, not meeting the expectations set by shame-based parenting, they develop a distorted self-perception. They may believe that their successes are undeserved or a result of luck rather than genuine competence. This distorted self-image becomes a breeding ground for impostor syndrome in adulthood. The internalisation of shame can lead individuals to question their worthiness, even in the face of objective achievements. Despite external validation, those with impostor syndrome may struggle to internalise a sense of accomplishment, attributing their successes to external factors rather than acknowledging their own capabilities.

Furthermore, the fear of being exposed as inadequate, which is a central component of impostor syndrome, mirrors the shame-inducing experiences of childhood. The persistent belief in one's inherent flaws, ingrained during early development, perpetuates a cycle of self-doubt and anxiety about being unmasked as undeserving of success. Impostor syndrome can affect various aspects of an individual's life, including their professional pursuits, relationships, and overall well-being. It may hinder career progression, limit the pursuit of challenging opportunities, and strain interpersonal connections as individuals grapple with the fear of being "found out."

The parent-child relationship, crucial for healthy social development, can be strained by shame-based parenting. Children may perceive their parents as judgmental and critical, compromising their ability to form secure and trusting relationships with others. Studies suggest a correlation between shame-based parenting and an increased risk of mental health issues in children. Conditions such as anxiety, depression, and personality disorders may be more prevalent among individuals who experience shame as a predominant form of discipline.

Shame-based parenting tends to focus on punishing undesirable behaviour rather than teaching problem-solving skills. Consequently, children raised in this environment may struggle to navigate challenges, lacking the constructive problem-solving mechanisms necessary for personal growth. In terms of behaviour, children raised with shame as a primary disciplinary tool may develop maladaptive coping mechanisms. These can manifest in various ways, such as aggression, withdrawal, or rebelliousness, as they grapple with the emotional turmoil associated with shame.

Recognising that you may be engaging in shame-based parenting is crucial for fostering a healthier approach to raising children. If your interactions predominantly involve criticism rather than praise, focusing on mistakes or shortcomings, it could be a sign of shame-based parenting. Pay attention to the language you use; if it tends to shame or humiliate your child, creating feelings of inherent inadequacy, this may indicate a shame-based approach.

Consider whether your love and approval seem contingent on your child's achievements or behaviours rather than being unconditional. If you constantly compare your child to others or set unreasonably high standards, it can create an environment of unrealistic expectations and foster feelings of inadequacy. Take note of how you handle your child's emotions. Dismissing or belittling their feelings can contribute to emotional suppression and a sense of shame. Similarly, using negative labels or name-calling reinforces shame-based tactics.

Reflect on your ability to empathise with your child's perspective. If you consistently prioritise discipline over understanding, it may contribute to a shame-based parenting dynamic. Be mindful of how you use affection; using it as a tool for compliance rather than expressing genuine love can create emotional deprivation. Finally, consider the balance in your interactions. If they primarily revolve around pointing out what your child has done wrong without offering positive reinforcement or guidance, it may indicate a reliance on shame-based tactics. Recognising these signs is the first step, and seeking support, such as parenting classes or counselling, can provide valuable insights and strategies for fostering a more nurturing and supportive environment for your child.

Breaking the cycle of negative behaviours is a profound journey that commences with introspection. Delve deeply into your parenting style, recognising and acknowledging the patterns that contribute to negative behaviours. Cultivating self-awareness becomes the foundational stepping stone toward fostering positive change. Transition the narrative from mere criticism of undesirable behaviours to the active reinforcement of positive actions. Actively praise and acknowledge your child's commendable conduct, constructing a robust framework of positive reinforcement. Establish clear and open channels of communication, fostering an environment where your child feels secure expressing their feelings and thoughts without the fear of judgment. Ensure that your expectations for your child are not only realistic but also age appropriate. Celebrate the small victories, setting the stage for a tangible and positive shift in behaviour. Consistently implement fair discipline, articulating rules and consequences with clarity and applying them consistently. This consistency provides a reliable framework for behaviour expectations.

Lead by example, embodying the positive behaviours you aspire to see in your child. Demonstrate virtues such as patience, empathy, and resilience, recognising the profound influence your actions hold. Impart problem-solving skills, encouraging your child to approach challenges critically and actively involving them in finding constructive solutions.

Craft a home environment that is not just supportive but nurturing, emphasising emotional security and providing a haven for expression. If breaking the cycle of negative behaviours proves to be a challenging task, it may indicate that you have been living in an environment characterised by shame. Consequently, unlearning the parenting patterns you have experienced can be difficult. In such cases, it is advisable to seek professional support from a therapist or parenting counsellor. Their expert guidance and customised tools can provide invaluable assistance in navigating and overcoming the challenges associated with breaking ingrained patterns.

Assist your child in developing emotional regulation skills, teaching them healthy coping mechanisms for handling frustration, disappointment, or anger. Empower them to manage their emotions autonomously, thereby diminishing the likelihood of negative outbursts. Dedicate quality time to engage with your child, participating in activities that foster bonding and positive connections, ultimately nurturing strong relationships built on trust and cooperation.

Breaking the cycle of negative behaviours is an incremental process that necessitates unwavering commitment, patience, and consistency. By seamlessly integrating these strategies into your parenting approach, you actively contribute to the creation of a positive and nurturing environment that not only supports but propels your child's growth and development.

Farzaneh Ghadirian

Chapter 12
The Impact of Trauma: Addressing Our Own and Our Children's Past Wounds

Enduring trauma has a deep and wide-reaching effect on people, leaving lasting marks in many parts of their lives. The aftermath goes beyond the obvious injuries, reaching into how they feel, think, act, and relate to others. Emotionally, trauma stirs up a mix of feelings. It can bring up haunting memories and flashbacks, like those experienced in Post-Traumatic Stress Disorder (PTSD). Anxiety becomes a constant presence, and the risk of depression casts a shadow over one's emotions. Mood swings, swinging between anger and sadness, resemble the ups and downs of turbulent weather.

In the realm of thinking, trauma disrupts the normal flow of thoughts. Concentrating becomes a tricky dance, stumbling under the weight of intrusive memories. Memory, once reliable, struggles to hold onto details or create new memories. In behaviour, trauma often leads to a story of avoidance and recklessness. People delicately navigate around reminders, as if being too close to the memories might unravel the fragile threads holding them together. Paradoxically, some might embrace risk and self-destructive habits, maybe as a way to escape or find some control in the chaos.

In relationships, the impact of trauma echoes in the challenges faced. Trust, a fragile bond, becomes rare and precious. Communication, the vital thread in connections, suffers as individuals grapple with unspoken pain. Social dynamics ebb and flow unevenly as avoidance and withdrawal become strategies to cope. So, the impact of trauma is not a single note but a symphony of difficulties, each note echoing through the corridors of a person's life. Trauma often gives rise to a range of emotional challenges. For adults, this might include symptoms of Post-Traumatic Stress Disorder (PTSD), anxiety, depression, and unpredictable mood swings. In children, these emotions may manifest through behavioural changes, withdrawal, or difficulty expressing their feelings.

In adults, the emotional aftermath of trauma can be intricate and multifaceted. Experiencing PTSD may involve persistent and distressing memories or flashbacks, making it challenging to navigate daily life. Anxiety becomes a pervasive companion, casting a shadow over even the most routine activities. The risk of depression looms, and mood swings can resemble turbulent weather patterns, with emotions fluctuating between anger and sorrow.

Children, on the other hand, may struggle to articulate their emotional turmoil. Behavioural changes can be a window into their inner world, with withdrawal or acting out being common responses. They may find it challenging to express their feelings verbally, resorting to behavioural cues that caregivers need to interpret.

Trauma disrupts our cognitive processes, affecting concentration and memory. For adults, the ability to focus might falter, and memories may become intrusive. Children may struggle academically or show signs of developmental delays due to cognitive disruptions. Cognitively, adults navigating trauma may experience difficulties in concentration, finding that their thoughts waltz erratically, mirroring the elusive steps of a dance. Memory, once a reliable companion, may falter, making it challenging to hold onto details or forge new recollections. In children, cognitive disruptions may be observed in academic settings. Their ability to concentrate on tasks might be compromised, impacting their learning experiences. Developmental delays can emerge, requiring a nuanced and patient approach to foster cognitive growth.

Both adults and children may develop specific behavioural patterns as a response to trauma. Adults might engage in avoidance or recklessness, trying to navigate a delicate balance between steering clear of triggers and embracing risk. Children may exhibit signs of hyperarousal or dissociation as they grapple with the impact of their experiences. The behavioural manifestations of trauma create intricate patterns that vary between adults and children. Adults may find themselves entangled in a narrative of avoidance, steering clear of reminders as if proximity might unravel the fragile threads holding them together. Simultaneously, some may embrace risk and self-destructive tendencies, perhaps seeking an escape or a semblance of control amidst the chaos. For children, behavioural responses may include signs of hyperarousal, where they are constantly on edge, alert to potential threats. Alternatively, dissociation might occur, a coping mechanism where they mentally detach from the overwhelming reality.

Trauma can strain interpersonal relationships. Trust, a fragile bond, becomes challenging to establish, and communication may suffer as unspoken pain creates barriers. In families, the dynamics may shift, with avoidance and withdrawal affecting the ebb and flow of connection. Interpersonal challenges stemming from trauma create a complex web of dynamics. Trust, a delicate bond easily fractured, may become a rare and precious commodity in relationships. Communication, the lifeline of connections, can be hampered as individuals grapple with the weight of unspoken pain. The ebb and flow of social dynamics may be disrupted, as avoidance and withdrawal take root. Addressing these intricate facets of trauma involves a combination of self-reflection, professional support, and intentional efforts to rebuild trust and connection. By understanding the nuanced impact of emotional, cognitive, and behavioural aspects, individuals can embark on a journey toward healing and resilience.

Trauma casts a profound shadow over the cognitive landscape, disrupting the intricate processes that shape our thoughts and memories. This disruption manifests in distinct ways for both adults and children, unveiling a complex tapestry of challenges. Trauma can significantly impact an adult's cognitive functioning, leading to difficulties in concentration and memory recall. The ability to focus may waver, resembling a delicate dance where the steps falter under the weight of intrusive memories. This lack of concentration can permeate various aspects of daily life, affecting work, relationships, and the ability to engage in routine activities. Intrusive memories often become an unwelcome companion, haunting the recesses of consciousness. These memories, vivid and distressing, may surface unexpectedly, disrupting the flow of thought and triggering emotional responses. The struggle to manage these intrusive thoughts adds an additional layer of complexity to the cognitive challenges faced by adults navigating the aftermath of trauma.

For children, the cognitive disruptions resulting from trauma can be particularly poignant, influencing their academic performance and overall developmental trajectory. The impact may manifest in struggles with concentration, making it challenging for them to engage effectively in learning environments. Academic challenges may become apparent as children grapple with the cognitive aftermath of trauma. Difficulty focusing on tasks, completing assignments, or participating in classroom activities can hinder their educational progress. The classroom, which should be a space for growth and exploration, can become a source of stress and frustration. Moreover, signs of developmental delays may emerge, affecting various domains such as language acquisition, motor skills, and social interactions. The cognitive disruptions experienced by traumatised children can create hurdles in their journey toward reaching developmental milestones.

The aftermath of trauma weaves a complex narrative of behavioural patterns, unveiling distinct responses in both adults and children. Many adults, in an effort to shield themselves from the distressing memories associated with trauma, may develop avoidance patterns. This involves steering clear of situations, places, or people that act as triggers. The avoidance is not merely a physical act but extends to emotional and psychological realms, as individuals strive to create a protective buffer against potential reminders of their traumatic past. Paradoxically, some adults may embrace risk and engage in reckless behaviour as a means of exerting control or seeking an escape from the emotional turmoil within. This recklessness can manifest in various ways, such as impulsive decision-making, substance abuse, or engaging in activities with little regard for personal safety.

In another hand, children, too, exhibit specific behavioural patterns in response to trauma, providing glimpses into the profound impact on their emotional and psychological well-being. Some children may display heightened levels of arousal, characterised by increased sensitivity to stimuli and a constant state of alertness. This hyperarousal is a manifestation of the heightened stress response triggered by traumatic experiences. These children may be easily startled, struggle with sleep disturbances, and find it challenging to concentrate.

On the other end of the spectrum, some children may adopt a coping mechanism known as dissociation. This involves mentally disconnecting from the present moment to shield themselves from the overwhelming emotions associated with trauma. Dissociation can manifest as spacing out, appearing emotionally detached, or struggling to engage with their surroundings.

In families, trauma can instigate shifts in dynamics, disrupting the ebb and flow of connection. Members may respond to trauma differently, leading to a complex interplay of avoidance and withdrawal. Some may retreat inward, grappling with their emotions in solitude, while others may inadvertently distance themselves from loved ones. Navigating the echoes of our own past wounds is a nuanced and multifaceted journey that demands a thoughtful approach. Embarking on this path involves intentional steps aimed at fostering self-awareness, acceptance, and ultimately, healing.

Initiating the process of healing requires a moment of self-reflection—a conscious effort to identify moments of trauma and the emotions entwined with them. Taking the time to explore the depths of our experiences lays the foundation for understanding the impact of past wounds on our present selves.

Crucial to the healing journey is acceptance—acknowledging the existence of past wounds and embracing them as integral parts of our life story. This acknowledgment is not an endorsement of pain but a courageous step towards allowing healing to take place. Seeking professional support, such as therapy or counselling, provides a structured and supportive environment for exploring and processing past traumas. The guidance of a mental health professional facilitates a deeper understanding of the roots of our pain and equips us with coping mechanisms to navigate the healing process.

Journaling serves as a powerful therapeutic outlet, providing a medium for us to express and make sense of our experiences. Putting pen to paper can be a cathartic process, allowing emotions to be articulated and gradually released, contributing to the unburdening of past wounds. Incorporating mindfulness and meditation practices into our routine contributes to staying present and cultivating self-awareness. These techniques provide valuable tools for managing overwhelming emotions, fostering a sense of calm, and creating a space for self-discovery.

A cornerstone of the healing journey is self-compassion. Treating ourselves with kindness, understanding, and patience becomes instrumental in navigating the challenges of self-recovery. Embracing self-compassion allows us to counteract self-blame and judgment, fostering an environment conducive to healing. Establishing and maintaining healthy boundaries is crucial for protection against potential triggers. Identifying situations, environments, or relationships that may exacerbate past wounds enables us to create a supportive space for personal growth and healing. Recognising and addressing the wounds borne by our children demands atonement for their unique needs, behaviours, and emotions. The journey involves creating a safe and supportive environment, seeking professional guidance, and gradually guiding them towards a path of healing.

Building a safe space for open communication is paramount. Encouraging children to express their feelings, thoughts, and concerns fosters an environment where they feel heard and validated. Listening actively and without judgment establishes a foundation for trust.

Seeking professional support, such as child therapy, can offer specialised guidance tailored to the unique needs of young minds. Child therapists are equipped to navigate the complexities of childhood trauma and provide age-appropriate interventions.

Approaching triggers cautiously and respecting the child's readiness is essential. Gradual exposure, coupled with age-appropriate expression of feelings through activities like art or play, provides children with alternative avenues for communicating and processing their experiences. Addressing our own and our children's wounds is a shared journey—one that requires patience, compassion, and a commitment to creating an environment conducive to healing and growth. By navigating these paths with intentionality and care, individuals and families can embark on a collective voyage toward resilience and well-being.

Farzaneh Ghadirian

Chapter 13
The Power of Forgiveness: Healing Relationships and Promoting Positive Behaviour

The power of forgiveness is transformative and liberating. At its core, forgiveness is the act of releasing oneself from the grip of negative emotions tied to a past offence or harm caused by others. It does not excuse the wrongdoing but rather frees the forgiver from the heavy burden of resentment and anger. Forgiveness holds the key to emotional liberation. By letting go of bitterness, individuals experience a profound sense of peace and emotional well-being. It serves as a healing balm for wounds inflicted by past actions, offering the opportunity for psychological and spiritual recovery. In the realm of interpersonal relationships, forgiveness is a powerful agent of reconciliation. It opens doors to rebuilding trust and understanding, fostering the potential for stronger and healthier connections. Choosing forgiveness is an act of personal growth, demanding resilience, empathy, and a willingness to move beyond pain.

Forgiveness contributes to reducing stress and resentment. The act of harbouring grudges can lead to increased negativity, and forgiveness alleviates these burdens, promoting improved mental and emotional well-being. It breaks the cycle of hurt and retaliation, introducing a positive force that can influence others and create a more compassionate environment. Choosing forgiveness is an empowering decision. It allows the forgiver to reclaim control over their emotional state and responses, demonstrating strength and resilience in the face of adversity. For many, forgiveness is tied to spiritual or moral values, reflecting a commitment to principles of compassion, mercy, and understanding.

While the journey of forgiveness can be challenging, its acknowledgment inspires individuals to embark on a path of emotional freedom, healing, and the restoration of relationships. Ultimately, forgiveness is a profound gift one gives to oneself, opening the door to a more positive and fulfilling life. Forgiving someone who has hurt you can be an immensely challenging endeavour, rooted in the complexity of human emotions and the profound impact of the inflicted pain. Several factors contribute to the difficulty of extending forgiveness.

The emotional aftermath of an offence often leaves deep scars. The hurt, betrayal, or trauma caused by someone's actions can evoke intense and enduring emotions. Navigating these emotions is a complex process, and the idea of forgiveness can seem inconceivable when wounds are still fresh. Moreover, the act of forgiveness is not synonymous with condoning or forgetting the wrongdoing. It's a nuanced process that requires individuals to confront the reality of the harm inflicted upon them. Reconciling the desire to forgive with the need for acknowledgment and justice adds layers of complexity to the forgiveness journey. Additionally, a sense of vulnerability can impede the forgiveness process. Opening oneself up to the possibility of being hurt again, and trusting the wrongdoer not to repeat the offence, requires courage and a willingness to be vulnerable. Fear of further pain or betrayal can be a significant barrier to extending forgiveness. Furthermore, forgiveness often intersects with one's sense of justice. The need for a fair and just response to wrongdoing can create internal conflicts when considering forgiveness. Striking a balance between acknowledging the severity of the offence and allowing space for forgiveness challenges individuals grappling with conflicting values. Cultural and societal influences also play a role. Societal expectations or cultural norms regarding justice and retribution can shape an individual's perception of forgiveness. In some contexts, forgiveness might be viewed as a sign of weakness or as letting the wrongdoer off the hook, making it harder for individuals to embrace forgiveness.

Forgiveness possesses a transformative power capable of healing relationships and fostering positive behaviour. Its influence extends beyond a mere act of absolution, permeating the emotional fabric of individuals and the dynamics of their interactions.

Forgiveness, as a potent balm for emotional wounds, operates as a profound catalyst in the intricate process of emotional healing. When individuals make the courageous choice to release resentment and let go of harboured grievances, they consciously carve out space within themselves for the restoration of emotional well-being. The act of forgiveness, akin to unlocking a door long guarded by anger's shackles, allows a flood of transformative emotions to enter. It is in this release of resentment that the heart finds liberation, shedding the weight of past grievances. This liberation, in turn, paves the way for a renewed sense of inner peace—a quietude that emanates from the healing depths of the emotional landscape. Emotional wounds, often concealed beneath layers of hurt and pain, find solace in the gentle embrace of forgiveness. It's a journey that involves acknowledging the depth of one's emotions, confronting the scars left by past experiences, and, ultimately, choosing to embrace the healing potential inherent in forgiveness. In this narrative of emotional healing, forgiveness becomes an active agent of change—an intentional step towards breaking free from the chains that bind one to the past. The emotional scars once tended to with forgiveness, transform into marks of resilience, testaments to the strength found in choosing compassion over lingering bitterness. As individuals traverse the path of forgiveness, they navigate the nuanced terrain of their emotions, allowing for a profound inner metamorphosis. This transformation extends beyond a mere cessation of negative feelings; it is a process of reclaiming emotional sovereignty, redefining the emotional landscape, and cultivating an environment where healing becomes not just a possibility but an inevitability. In essence, the journey of facilitating emotional healing through forgiveness is a testament to the human spirit's capacity for renewal and growth. It is a narrative of resilience, where the act of forgiveness becomes a guiding light, illuminating the path towards inner peace and emotional well-being.

Forgiveness, as a profound and transformative act, goes beyond the realm of personal absolution. It emerges as a powerful embodiment of empathy and understanding, demanding individuals to embark on a journey of deep emotional introspection.
At its core, forgiveness beckons individuals to empathise with the perspective of those who have caused harm. This empathetic engagement is not a dismissal of the pain endured but rather an acknowledgment of the complexities inherent in the human experience. It requires a willingness to comprehend the intricate interplay of circumstances, emotions, and personal struggles that might have driven someone to inflict harm.

In the process of extending empathy, forgiveness becomes a bridge to a deeper understanding of human fallibility. It invites individuals to recognise the shared vulnerability that unites us all. By acknowledging the inherent imperfections and struggles embedded in the human condition, forgiveness promotes a broader and more compassionate perspective. The act of forgiving is, in essence, an exercise in seeing beyond the immediate actions and delving into the complexities of what it means to be human. It challenges individuals to confront their capacity for mistakes and misjudgements, fostering a humility that transcends the boundaries of personal grievances.

Moreover, forgiveness serves as a catalyst for connection. As individuals navigate the landscape of understanding, they forge a profound connection with the shared humanity that binds us all. Compassion, then, becomes the cornerstone upon which forgiveness is built—a compassionate understanding that recognises the inherent frailties and challenges that define the human experience. In the tapestry of human relationships, forgiveness emerges not only as a personal release from resentment but as a powerful force that fosters empathy, understanding, and interconnectedness. It is an invitation to embrace the complexities of the human journey, forging a path toward healing that extends beyond the individual to encompass the collective fabric of shared experiences.

Forgiveness, as a transformative process, not only contributes to our healing but also plays a pivotal role in shaping the emotional landscape for our children, fostering an environment of healing and resilience. When adults embrace the journey of forgiveness, they actively model emotional resilience for the younger generation, offering a profound lesson in navigating life's challenges. Children observe firsthand the transformative power of choosing healing over holding onto pain. This modelling becomes a powerful legacy, imparting the invaluable skill of emotional resilience to the next generation. As adults navigate the complexities of forgiveness, demonstrating vulnerability and strength in the face of adversity, children learn that overcoming pain is not only possible but also a courageous and empowering choice. Witnessing this journey, they internalise the idea that resilience is not the absence of challenges but the capacity to confront and transcend them.

Moreover, this modelling of emotional resilience extends beyond forgiveness, influencing how children perceive and respond to difficulties in their own lives. It instils in them the understanding that setbacks and conflicts are inherent aspects of the human experience, and the ability to navigate these challenges with resilience is a valuable life skill. The lesson of forgiveness, intertwined with emotional resilience, becomes a beacon of hope and empowerment for the younger generation. It teaches them that healing is an ongoing process, a journey that requires courage, self-reflection, and a commitment to growth. Ultimately, this modelling shapes children into individuals who approach life's adversities with strength, adaptability, and a deep understanding of the transformative potential embedded in the act of forgiveness.

Forgiveness, when woven into the fabric of family life, becomes a cornerstone for cultivating a culture rooted in understanding and compassion. In families where forgiveness is not just a concept but a practised virtue, children absorb profound lessons in conflict resolution and emotional resilience. Growing up in an environment where forgiveness is valued, children learn to navigate conflicts with grace and empathy. They witness the transformative power of letting go of grievances and embracing understanding. This cultural shift away from holding grudges and harbouring resentment becomes a lasting legacy that children carry into their own relationships and interactions. Within this culture of forgiveness, conflicts are approached not as battlegrounds of blame but as opportunities for growth and understanding. Children, influenced by the forgiveness they've experienced and observed, develop a capacity for empathy, kindness, and the ability to extend grace to others. Moreover, this cultural foundation of forgiveness promotes healing over hostility. It teaches children that relationships are resilient and capable of weathering storms when nurtured by forgiveness and understanding. The practice of forgiveness, therefore, contributes not only to individual well-being but also to the creation of familial bonds steeped in love, resilience, and a commitment to mutual growth.

In many instances, the pain we carry is deeply embedded in generational patterns of hurt and resentment. When we make the conscious choice to forgive, we actively engage in breaking the chains of this generational pain. This intentional act becomes a profound gift we offer to our children, presenting them with an opportunity to inherit a different narrative—one characterised by healing rather than perpetuating the patterns of hurt that may have persisted through generations. Choosing forgiveness is, therefore, an act of courage that reverberates across family histories. It signals a departure from the script of pain and animosity, charting a new course for future generations. By breaking the cycle of generational hurt, we create space for a legacy built on resilience, understanding, and the transformative power of forgiveness. Our children, in witnessing this courageous choice, not only experience the immediate benefits of a more harmonious family environment but also inherit a blueprint for navigating challenges in their own lives. Breaking generational patterns through forgiveness becomes a beacon of hope, illuminating the path toward healthier, more connected relationships and offering our children the possibility of a brighter and more emotionally nourishing future.

Forgiveness serves as a profound manifestation of emotional intelligence—an essential skill encompassing the understanding and management of our own emotions while empathising with others. As we engage in the transformative process of forgiveness and healing, we actively pass on this invaluable emotional intelligence to our children. In the context of forgiveness, emotional intelligence involves recognising and processing our own emotions related to the hurt or harm we've experienced. It goes beyond mere forgiveness, encompassing the ability to empathise with the perspectives of those who may have caused us pain. This nuanced understanding and management of emotions contribute significantly to the healing process. By modelling forgiveness, we demonstrate to our children the intricate facets of emotional intelligence. They learn not only to identify and express their emotions authentically but also to navigate the complexities of interpersonal relationships with empathy and understanding. This transfer of emotional intelligence becomes a lasting legacy, equipping our children with the tools to build healthier connections, resolve conflicts constructively, and cultivate a more harmonious and emotionally rich life.

At last, the practice of forgiveness within familial relationships unfolds as a powerful blueprint for establishing and sustaining healthy dynamics. Children, as keen observers, witness the intricate process of how conflicts can be navigated and resolved through the transformative power of forgiveness, thoughtful communication, and genuine empathy.

In the family setting, forgiveness becomes a guiding light, illuminating the path toward resolution and healing. The visible demonstration of choosing forgiveness over resentment or animosity provides children with a tangible example of how challenges can be faced and overcome within the context of relationships. This familial model serves as a template for our children's own relationships, both within the family unit and beyond. Armed with the understanding that forgiveness is a fundamental element in the fabric of healthy connections, they are equipped to approach conflicts with a mindset of reconciliation and understanding. Thus, the practice of forgiveness not only heals individual hearts but also contributes to the creation of a legacy—a legacy of resilient, empathetic, and harmonious relationships that extend beyond the boundaries of one generation, fostering positive connections in the tapestry of family life.

Farzaneh Ghadirian

Chapter 14
The Role of Discipline in Shaping Behaviour: Finding a Balance Between Structure and Compassion

The role of discipline in shaping behaviour is a delicate dance between providing structure and demonstrating compassion. Striking the right balance between these elements is essential for fostering positive development in individuals. Discipline, when approached with both firmness and understanding, becomes a guiding force that shapes behaviour and instils values. Discipline serves as the framework within which individuals learn to navigate societal norms and expectations. It provides a set of boundaries that define acceptable behaviour, offering a sense of security and predictability. This structure is crucial in helping individuals understand the consequences of their actions and fostering a sense of responsibility. However, discipline should not be synonymous with harshness or rigidity. Compassion plays a pivotal role in effective discipline. Understanding the unique needs, emotions, and motivations of individuals allows for a more empathetic approach. Instead of focusing solely on punitive measures, compassionate discipline seeks to address the root causes of behaviour and guide individuals toward positive alternatives.

Discipline is a concept that originates from the Latin word "disciplina," which means instruction or knowledge. In the context of human behaviour, discipline refers to the practice of training individuals to follow a code of conduct, adhere to rules, and develop self-control. It encompasses the guidance, correction, and regulation of behaviour to achieve specific goals or standards. The role of discipline in parenting is multifaceted, encompassing the guidance, correction, and nurturing of a child's behaviour to foster their overall development.

Discipline helps parents set clear boundaries and expectations for their children. Establishing rules and limits provides a structured environment that helps children understand acceptable behaviour, creating a sense of security and predictability. This sense of structure is crucial for children as it provides a framework within which they can navigate and comprehend the world around them. Clearly defined boundaries offer guidance, shaping their understanding of what is acceptable and fostering a secure environment that promotes healthy development. In the absence of well-established boundaries, children may feel uncertain about expectations, leading to confusion and potential behavioural challenges. The role of discipline, in this context, is not just corrective but proactive, creating a foundation for positive behaviour and emotional well-being. As parents consistently enforce boundaries with love and understanding, children internalise these expectations, contributing to their overall growth and the development of a strong parent-child relationship. Through the application of discipline, parents play a crucial role in imparting fundamental values and morals to their children.

Discipline serves as a guiding force, aligning actions with virtues essential for a child's moral development. In this intricate process, parents consciously integrate teachings of empathy, respect, responsibility, and other virtues into disciplinary actions. The objective is not merely correction but a profound shaping of the child's character, fostering qualities that contribute to their ethical understanding and compassionate engagement with the world. This intentional alignment of discipline with values goes beyond rule enforcement. It involves a continuous dialogue and demonstration of virtuous behaviour, creating a holistic approach that integrates moral principles into everyday actions. The outcome is a child who not only understands societal norms but embodies the deeper values that underpin harmonious human interactions. In essence, discipline becomes a vehicle for instilling a moral compass, and navigating children towards becoming individuals of integrity, empathy, and ethical conduct.

Discipline, as a guiding force in parenting, actively promotes responsibility among children by instilling a profound understanding of accountability. Through the imposition of consequences for their actions, children embark on a crucial journey of cause and effect. This firsthand experience becomes a dynamic classroom where they glean insights into the repercussions of their choices. Within this framework, discipline becomes a powerful teacher, imparting invaluable lessons about the significance of accountability and the art of decision-making. As children navigate the consequences of their behaviour, they develop a heightened awareness of the impact their actions can have on themselves and others. This process not only fosters a sense of responsibility but also equips them with the tools to make thoughtful and accountable choices in various aspects of their lives. Ultimately, discipline becomes a transformative vehicle for cultivating a profound sense of responsibility in the growing minds of children.

In the realm of parenting, effective discipline emerges as a potent catalyst for nurturing a child's self-control and emotional regulation. This transformative process unfolds as children engage in the essential journey of learning to manage impulses and express emotions appropriately. At its core, discipline becomes a guide, offering valuable lessons in emotional intelligence. Children, through the structure of discipline, develop a heightened awareness of their impulses and emotions. They navigate the delicate balance of acknowledging and understanding these internal states while acquiring the skills to express them in socially acceptable ways. This journey of self-control is foundational, contributing significantly to a child's social and emotional well-being. Discipline, when wielded as a tool for fostering self-regulation, equips children with the resilience and adaptability needed to navigate the complexities of interpersonal relationships and emotional landscapes. In essence, effective discipline becomes a roadmap guiding children towards the development of crucial life skills that form the bedrock of their holistic well-being.

Positive behaviour modelling is a deliberate and transformative approach in parenting, focusing on the celebration of virtuous actions rather than solely correcting missteps. This method

involves actively praising and rewarding positive behaviour, creating a dynamic environment where children are celebrated for their virtues. The essence of this approach lies in shining a spotlight on the positive aspects of a child's behaviour. Rather than being solely recipients of correction, children become active participants in a journey of affirmation and growth.
Encouragement becomes a potent motivator, inspiring children not only to adopt positive behaviours but to internalise them as integral aspects of their character. Within this paradigm, discipline undergoes a significant transformation. It evolves into a tool that not only corrects deviations but, more importantly, shapes the trajectory of a child's conduct. This is achieved by fostering a culture where positivity is not only recognised but celebrated and woven into the fabric of daily life. The encouragement of positive behaviour, facilitated by effective discipline, emerges as a crucial factor in cultivating a child's character and establishing a home environment rooted in affirmation and growth.

Fostering independence is a way for children to learn to follow rules and make choices within established boundaries. This process instils in them a sense of autonomy and confidence in their decision-making abilities. Through the guidance of discipline, children navigate the space between rules and choices, developing valuable skills that contribute to their overall growth and self-reliance. By providing a framework for decision-making within defined limits, discipline becomes a crucial tool in nurturing a child's independence. It offers them the opportunity to understand the consequences of their choices, fostering a sense of responsibility and ownership over their actions. In this way, discipline becomes a guiding force, shaping not only behaviour but also the development of essential life skills.

Discipline is a powerful teacher, imparting crucial lessons about consequences to children. Through both positive and negative consequences, children gain a profound understanding of how their actions impact themselves and those around them. This experiential learning becomes a cornerstone for the development of empathy and social skills.

When discipline involves positive consequences for desirable behaviour, children learn the intrinsic rewards of making good choices. This positive reinforcement creates a connection between actions and positive outcomes, motivating children to repeat these behaviours. On the flip side, experiencing negative consequences for undesirable behaviour teaches them about accountability and the effects of their actions on themselves and others. The lessons learned through discipline contribute significantly to the development of empathy. Understanding the consequences of one's actions cultivates a heightened awareness of how behaviour influences the feelings and experiences of others. This, in turn, lays the foundation for the development of strong social skills, as children learn to navigate relationships with sensitivity and consideration for others' well-being. In essence, discipline becomes a dynamic tool for shaping behaviour and character by providing real-world experiences that guide children toward responsible, empathetic, and socially adept individuals. Through these lessons in consequence, children not only understand the impact of their actions but also acquire the skills to navigate the complex web of social interactions with compassion and understanding.

Effective discipline is not a one-size-fits-all approach but a dynamic and responsive strategy that evolves alongside a child's developmental journey. Recognising and adapting to the unique needs, capabilities, and challenges of each developmental stage is essential for successful parenting. During the early stages of life, infants and toddlers are navigating a world of exploration. Effective discipline involves creating a safe and stimulating environment while setting gentle boundaries. Consistency and repetition are key as young children thrive on routine. Simple redirection and positive reinforcement lay the foundation for understanding acceptable behaviour.

As children enter the preschool years, their curiosity expands, and they begin to test boundaries. Discipline at this stage involves clear communication of expectations, using simple explanations for rules. Reinforcing positive behaviour with praise and small rewards helps shape their understanding of right and wrong.

Discipline for school-age children becomes more complex as they engage with peers and societal norms. Clear rules and consequences should be established, involving children in the decision-making process when appropriate. Discussions about actions and consequences become valuable, fostering a sense of responsibility. Encouraging self-expression and problem-solving skills is crucial during this stage.

Teenagers are navigating the challenges of identity, independence, and peer influence. Effective discipline requires open communication, active listening, and negotiation. Consequences should be fair and discussed in advance, allowing teenagers to understand the reasoning behind the rules. Encouraging autonomy while providing guidance becomes central to successful discipline during adolescence. Throughout these developmental stages, the underlying principles of effective discipline include consistency, positive reinforcement, and a focus on teaching rather than punitive measures. Recognising that children's capacities and needs change over time allows parents to tailor their disciplinary approaches, creating an environment that supports the child's evolving understanding of the world and their place in it.

Effective discipline is not solely about correction; it is a powerful tool for building and strengthening the parent-child relationship. When approached with warmth, consistency, and a foundation of mutual respect, discipline becomes a means of fostering a deep and meaningful connection between parents and children. Communication is the cornerstone of a strong parent-child connection. Clearly articulating expectations, rules, and consequences ensures that children understand what is expected of them. Open and honest communication also allows children to express themselves, fostering a sense of being heard and understood. Respect forms the basis of a healthy parent-child relationship. Effective discipline involves treating children with dignity, acknowledging their perspectives, and valuing their feelings. When discipline is administered with respect, it reinforces the idea that rules are in place for their well-being and growth. Consistency in discipline creates a stable and predictable environment. When children know what to expect, they feel secure and are more likely to trust their parents. Consistent application of rules and consequences builds a sense of reliability, contributing to the establishment of a strong parent-child bond.

While discipline often involves addressing challenging behaviours, incorporating positive reinforcement is equally crucial. Celebrating and acknowledging positive behaviour strengthens the parent-child connection. This positive reinforcement can take the form of verbal praise, small rewards, or quality time spent together. Effective discipline requires emotional availability from parents. Being attuned to a child's emotions, both positive and negative, fosters a deeper understanding of their needs. Providing emotional support during moments of discipline contributes to a sense of security and trust in the parent-child relationship. Discipline, when viewed as a teaching opportunity, becomes a way to impart valuable life lessons. Explaining the reasons behind rules and consequences helps children understand the importance of responsibility and accountability. These teaching moments strengthen the parent-child connection by creating a shared understanding.

Understanding the Root Causes of Discipline-related Struggles

Parents who have faced past hardships or trauma often encounter challenges in establishing disciplined role models for their children. The lasting impact of unresolved trauma can manifest in various ways, significantly affecting their ability to regulate emotions, respond calmly to challenges, and maintain consistent discipline. The lingering effects of their own difficult experiences may create barriers, hindering their capacity to serve as effective role models. Unresolved trauma can contribute to emotional distress, making it difficult for parents to navigate the complexities of discipline with the patience and consistency needed for positive modelling. As a result, the cycle of unaddressed trauma may inadvertently influence the parent-child dynamic, emphasising the importance of recognising and addressing past experiences for the well-being of both parents and children. Growing up without positive role models in terms of discipline can indeed contribute to a cycle of ineffective parenting. When individuals have not witnessed healthy disciplinary practices during their formative years, they may encounter challenges in emulating such behaviours when they transition into parenthood. The absence of positive role models deprives them of firsthand experience in observing how effective discipline can be implemented with a balance of structure and compassion. In such cases, individuals may grapple with uncertainty about what constitutes healthy discipline. The lack of exposure to positive examples might lead them to default to either overly harsh enforcement or leniency, struggling to find the elusive sweet spot between the two. Additionally, the absence of positive role models may leave individuals without a solid foundation for understanding the nuances of effective communication, consistency, and empathy in the realm of discipline.

This deficiency in positive role modelling can perpetuate a cycle where ineffective disciplinary patterns are passed down through generations. Without a reference point for constructive discipline, individuals may resort to methods that they witnessed, even if those methods are less than ideal. As a result, the cycle continues, and children raised in such environments may face challenges in developing effective discipline strategies when they become parents. Breaking this cycle requires a conscious effort to seek alternative models and resources that provide insights into healthy discipline. It involves a commitment to learning and understanding the fundamental principles of effective discipline, incorporating elements of structure, clear communication, and empathy. Recognising the impact of the lack of positive role models is the first step toward breaking free from the cycle and fostering a nurturing and supportive environment for the next generation.

Inconsistency in parenting styles can be a challenging hurdle for both parents and children to navigate. When parents grapple with finding the right balance between harsh enforcement and punishment, it often results in an unpredictable and inconsistent approach to discipline. This inconsistency can create confusion for children, as the expectations and consequences may appear ambiguous or constantly shifting. The struggle to strike a balance may stem from a variety of factors, such as a lack of clear disciplinary guidelines or uncertainty about the most effective methods of correction. Parents facing this challenge might resort to different disciplinary tactics depending on their emotional state, the severity of the situation, or external stressors. As a result, children may find it difficult to understand and internalise the expected behaviours, leading to a sense of unpredictability and insecurity. Inconsistent parenting styles can impact a child's ability to develop a clear understanding of boundaries and expectations. The lack of a cohesive and reliable disciplinary framework may hinder the formation of a stable foundation for behavioural norms. Children may struggle to grasp the connection between actions and consequences when faced with inconsistent responses from their parents.

The lack of formal education or guidance on effective parenting strategies can pose a significant challenge for some parents. In the absence of the necessary tools and knowledge, individuals may find themselves ill-equipped to navigate the complexities of parenting, particularly in the realm of discipline. This absence of essential skills can lead to the adoption of ineffective or inconsistent disciplinary approaches, ultimately hindering their ability to serve as positive role models for their children. Parents who haven't received formal education in parenting may struggle to understand age-appropriate disciplinary techniques, communication strategies, and methods to foster positive behaviour. The absence of this knowledge can result in a reliance on punitive measures or arbitrary enforcement, contributing to a lack of consistency in their disciplinary approach.

Moreover, the absence of parenting education may leave parents feeling uncertain about the most suitable methods for addressing behavioural issues or instilling values in their children. This uncertainty can manifest in a range of disciplinary inconsistencies, as parents may experiment with different approaches without a clear understanding of their potential impact.

The demands of parenting, coupled with external life stressors, can create a formidable challenge for individuals, often leading to feelings of overwhelm. Parents navigating high levels of stress may encounter difficulties in maintaining consistent discipline within the family dynamic. Various stressors, such as financial pressures, demanding work environments, or personal challenges, can significantly impact emotional resilience, subsequently affecting the ability to model effective discipline. The weight of stress can impede parents from responding to their children's behaviours in a measured and consistent manner. When overwhelmed, individuals may find it challenging to regulate their emotions, making it more likely that disciplinary actions will be reactive rather than thoughtful. This reactive approach can contribute to inconsistencies in discipline, as the response to similar behaviours may vary based on the parent's emotional state at any given moment. Moreover, chronic stress can affect cognitive functions related to decision-making and problem-solving. Parents under prolonged stress may struggle to devise and implement consistent disciplinary strategies, further exacerbating challenges in maintaining a stable and predictable disciplinary environment for their children.

Cultural and societal influences exert a significant impact on the formulation of parenting styles, shaping how individuals approach discipline within their families. The prevailing cultural norms and societal expectations within a given community can profoundly influence a parent's perspective on disciplinary measures. In certain cultural contexts, there may be a tendency to prioritise punitive approaches over positive and constructive methods of discipline. This inclination might stem from deeply ingrained beliefs about the role of authority, obedience, and the perceived effectiveness of strict disciplinary measures. Parents may find themselves adhering to traditional practices that have been passed down through generations, even if these methods are not necessarily aligned with contemporary understandings of effective discipline. Societal expectations, too, contribute to the overarching narrative around parenting and discipline. Pressures from external sources, such as media representations or community standards, can influence parents' choices in how they choose to enforce discipline. The desire to conform to societal expectations or norms may lead parents to adopt certain disciplinary practices, even if these methods are not reflective of their personal beliefs or preferences.

Chapter 15
The Importance of Self-Care for Parents: Maintaining Our Own Mental Health to Better Support Our Kids

Self-care refers to the deliberate and conscious actions individuals take to prioritise their physical, mental, and emotional well-being. It involves activities and practices that promote personal health, reduce stress, and contribute to a sense of balance and fulfilment. Self-care is a proactive approach to maintaining one's overall wellness, recognising the importance of taking time for oneself amid life's demands and responsibilities. Self-care activities can vary widely and are unique to each person, as what works for one individual may not be suitable for another. Common self-care practices include adequate sleep, regular exercise, a balanced diet, mindfulness and meditation, spending time in nature, engaging in hobbies, setting boundaries, and fostering positive social connections. The concept of self-care emphasises the understanding that attending to one's own needs is not selfish but, in fact, essential for sustained well-being. It involves making intentional choices that prioritise health and happiness, contributing to increased resilience and the ability to navigate life's challenges more effectively. Self-care is a fundamental aspect of maintaining a healthy and fulfilling life, promoting a holistic approach to overall wellness.

Parenting, a delicate juggling act of meeting children's needs while managing our own, hinges on the critical practice of self-care. When we, as parents, intentionally prioritise our well-being, it transforms the way we navigate the multifaceted demands of raising a family. This intentional act isn't a self-indulgent luxury; it's a strategic investment in the harmony of our family unit. By acknowledging our personal needs and engaging in activities that replenish us, we ensure we have the energy, emotional stability, and mental clarity required to meet the diverse needs of our children. Self-care isn't merely about occasional treats; it's a continuous, mindful act of carving out time for us. This intentional practice equips us with the tools necessary to navigate the unpredictable twists of parenting. Patience becomes a wellspring that allows us to respond to challenges with calmness, resilience acts as a shield against inevitable difficulties, and a positive mindset becomes our guiding compass, illuminating joys amidst responsibilities.

Parental burnout stands as one of the most formidable challenges in the realm of parenting, a relentless adversary that can leave even the most dedicated caregivers feeling drained and overwhelmed. It's a persistent risk, fuelled by the continuous demands of raising children, managing households, and navigating the complexities of family life. The importance of self-care in preventing burnout cannot be overstated. Regular and intentional self-care routines become a lifeline, a proactive measure that helps parents recharge their physical, emotional, and mental reserves. Amid constant responsibilities, these routines offer a sanctuary where parents can momentarily step back, replenish their energy, and regain a sense of balance.

Self-care acts as a buffer against the insidious encroachment of burnout by addressing its root causes. For many parents, burnout emerges when the scales tip too heavily toward giving and nurturing without receiving adequate replenishment. It's akin to pouring from an empty cup, a scenario that depletes energy, diminishes resilience, and erodes the joy inherent in parenting. The roots of burnout in parenting are deeply entwined with the complexities of modern life and the inherent challenges of raising children. From the tender care demanded by infants to the nuanced navigation of the emotional landscape of teenagers, each developmental stage comes with its own set of challenges. The constant juggling act, without adequate pauses for respite, can gradually lead to emotional exhaustion. The demands start early, with the around-the-clock care needed for infants. The sleepless nights, the ever-present vigilance, and the sheer physical demands of caring for a newborn can be overwhelming. As children grow, so do the demands, evolving into a multifaceted array of responsibilities. From attending to academic and extracurricular needs to providing emotional support during tumultuous teenage years, the roles and expectations placed on parents can feel ceaseless.

The cycle of meeting these demands without sufficient breaks creates a stress loop. Parents may find themselves caught in a rhythm where moments of relaxation are rare, and the weight of responsibilities becomes a constant companion. Emotional exhaustion can set in as the demands persist, impacting both the mental and physical well-being of parents. In this intricate dance, finding moments to step back, breathe, and replenish becomes essential to navigate the unrelenting demands of parenting with resilience and well-being.

Another significant contributor to parental burnout is the lack of adequate support systems. Parenting is a complex journey, and having a robust support network, whether from a partner, family, or community, is essential to share the burdens and joys of the experience. When this support is lacking, parents may find themselves navigating the challenges of parenthood in isolation. Feeling alone in the responsibilities of parenting can intensify the burdens. The absence of someone to share the load, help, or provide emotional support can contribute to burnout. It's akin to carrying the weight of parenting entirely on one's shoulders, with no one to help distribute the load. The sense of isolation can manifest in various ways, from the daily tasks of childcare to the emotional challenges of parenting. Without a support system to turn to, parents may experience a heightened sense of pressure, amplifying the stress associated with meeting the demands of parenting. Building a supportive community and seeking assistance when needed are crucial strategies to counteract the impact of insufficient support and mitigate the risk of burnout.

Parental burnout can also stem from the weight of high expectations and pressure. Whether these expectations are self-imposed or influenced by societal standards, the pursuit of perfection in both parenting and personal life can exert tremendous pressure on individuals.

The desire to meet unrealistic standards can create a constant sense of inadequacy and stress. Parents may feel compelled to excel in every aspect of their roles, striving to be the ideal caregiver, partner, and professional simultaneously. This unrelenting pursuit of perfection, often fuelled by societal ideals and the comparison trap, can contribute significantly to the development of burnout. The pressure to balance various responsibilities and roles while maintaining an image of success can be overwhelming. Parents may find themselves caught in a cycle of striving for unattainable standards, leading to increased stress and the depletion of emotional reserves.

Burnout can result from neglecting self-care, a common pitfall for many parents who prioritise the well-being of their children above their own. In the relentless pursuit of meeting their children's needs, parents may inadvertently overlook essential self-care practices. Neglecting to recharge and replenish physical, emotional, and mental reserves creates a vulnerable state where burnout can take root. The continuous cycle of caregiving without adequate moments for personal rejuvenation can lead to emotional exhaustion and diminished resilience. Parents may find themselves caught in a perpetual loop of meeting the demands of parenting without dedicating time and attention to their own well-being. This neglect of self-care not only compromises the parent's health but also diminishes their capacity to navigate the challenges of parenting with patience and resilience.

The impact of past trauma can significantly contribute to parental burnout. Parents who have experienced trauma may carry unresolved emotional burdens that can be triggered or exacerbated by the challenges of parenting. Past traumas create a heightened vulnerability, and the stresses of parenting may act as a catalyst for the re-emergence of unresolved issues. The emotional toll of navigating parenthood alongside unhealed wounds can amplify the risk of burnout. These parents may find themselves grappling not only with the typical challenges of raising children but also with the resurfacing of past traumas. The intricate interplay between unresolved emotional burdens and the demands of parenting can create a profound and enduring impact, increasing the likelihood of burnout.

Guilt and perfectionism are significant contributors to parental burnout. The pervasive influence of societal expectations, coupled with comparisons to other parents, often fuels feelings of guilt among individuals navigating the challenges of parenthood. Striving for an unattainable standard of perfection can create a continuous cycle of stress, gradually eroding the joy inherent in the parenting journey. Parents may find themselves grappling with the weight of guilt, questioning their decisions, and internalising societal pressures. The constant pursuit of perfection can lead to heightened stress levels, making it challenging to fully appreciate the moments of joy and connection with their children. Addressing these complex emotions involves a shift in mindset, recognising that perfection is an unrealistic goal and that embracing imperfections is an inherent part of the parenting experience. Cultivating self-compassion and acknowledging that every parent faces unique challenges can serve as a powerful antidote to the toxic combination of guilt and perfectionism that contributes to parental burnout.

Lack of boundaries is a noteworthy factor contributing to parental burnout. The increasing integration of technology in our lives, coupled with blurred lines between work and personal time, creates challenges for parents trying to establish clear boundaries. The constant connectivity makes it difficult for parents to fully disconnect, fostering a sense of being always "on" and perpetuating the cycle of burnout. The pervasive nature of digital devices and the expectation of constant availability can intrude upon precious moments of personal and family time. Parents may find it challenging to carve out dedicated moments for relaxation and rejuvenation, further intensifying the risk of burnout.

Work-life imbalance poses a significant and enduring challenge that markedly contributes to parental burnout. The ongoing juggling act between the demands of work and family life creates a precarious situation for numerous parents. Factors such as heavy workloads, prolonged working hours, and the pursuit of a harmonious work-life balance compound the stress experienced by parents. The weight of high workloads and demanding job responsibilities often leads parents to invest considerable time and energy in their professional obligations. However, when this dedication to work-related commitments lacks a counterbalance with ample time for personal and family life, it fosters a pervasive sense of overwhelm and exhaustion. Extended working hours, frequently extending beyond the conventional 9-to-5 framework, further diminish the time available for rest, relaxation, and meaningful interactions with family members. The perpetual struggle to achieve a harmonious work-life balance establishes a cyclical pattern of stress, impacting both the professional and personal spheres of life.

Embarking on the journey to overcome burnout feels like delving into the depths of your own soul—a profound exploration where the tender care of your well-being becomes the guiding light through life's intricate challenges. These strategies are not just guidelines; they are compassionate companions, walking beside you through the storm of life's demands.

Imagine self-care as a gentle, healing touch for your weary spirit. Immerse yourself in activities that resonate with the core of who you are—whether it's the therapeutic dance of exercise, the comforting escape of a good book, or the grounding embrace of nature. Let self-care evolve into a sacred ritual, a nurturing balm for your soul. Picture boundaries as protective shields around your inner sanctuary. Create clear distinctions between the demands of work and the sacred space of your personal life. Allocate specific times for work commitments and fiercely guard moments for yourself and your loved ones. In establishing these boundaries, you carve out havens of tranquillity amidst life's chaotic rhythm.

Visualise delegation as a shared journey, lightening the burden that weighs upon you. Don't hesitate to seek support from those around you—colleagues, friends, and family. In sharing responsibilities, you transform isolation into collaboration, and the load becomes feathers carried away by a gentle breeze. Envision prioritisation as an artist sculpting order from the chaos of life. Evaluate tasks based on their significance and urgency. Organise your responsibilities into manageable fragments, turning even the most overwhelming challenges into stepping stones along the river of your journey.

Think of time management as your graceful dance partner, guiding you through life's demands with poise. Plan your day with intention, setting realistic goals and avoiding the alluring call of overcommitment. Mindfully allocate moments for rest, honouring the natural ebb and flow of your energy. Imagine seeking professional help as a gentle guide accompanying you on your challenging expedition. If burnout casts a shadow on your well-being, consider the nurturing support of a therapist, counsellor, or coach. Their wisdom becomes a beacon of resilience and coping strategies, a comforting presence on your journey.

Reflect on your goals as constellations in the night sky, ensuring they align with the compass of your values. If the stars lose their lustre, don't hesitate to adjust your course. Reducing unnecessary stress becomes a celestial recalibration, a renewed commitment to your well-being. Envision saying "no" as a powerful act of self-preservation—a firm yet compassionate declaration of your boundaries. Recognise your limitations and wield this power with grace. Saying no, when necessary, becomes a statement of self-worth and a shield against burnout.

Rediscover the joy of hobbies as vibrant hues splash across the canvas of your life. Engage in activities that bring joy and fulfilment outside the realm of work. Cultivating hobbies becomes the antidote to monotony and a celebration of your multifaceted self.

Integrate mindfulness into your daily life as a gentle breeze carrying away the stress of the day. Embrace practices such as deep breathing, yoga, or mindfulness meditation. Let these moments of mindfulness become anchors of serenity amid life's tempests.

As you navigate the landscape of addressing burnout, remember that it is an ongoing journey. Prioritising self-care and well-being are not a destination but a continuous commitment to your resilience and flourishing. Embrace these strategies as compassionate companions on your odyssey, guiding you towards a life of balance, joy, and fulfilment.

Chapter 16
The Long-Term Impact of Blind Spots: Recognising the Consequences for Future Generations

The long-term impact of blind spots can be profound, affecting various aspects of personal and professional life. Blind spots, which refer to areas of unawareness or ignorance, can hinder growth, relationships, and overall well-being.

In the realm of personal development, blind spots can manifest as a limited understanding of one's strengths and weaknesses. Without a clear awareness of these attributes, individuals may struggle to identify areas for improvement or recognise opportunities for personal growth. For instance, someone might underestimate their leadership potential, hindering them from taking on leadership roles that could enhance their skills and broaden their experiences. On the professional front, blind spots can obscure the pathways to career advancement. This might occur when an individual fails to recognise the skills or qualifications necessary for a promotion or new role. The inability to identify and address these blind spots can result in stagnation or missed opportunities for climbing the career ladder. Skill enhancement is another area affected by blind spots. Individuals may have talents or abilities that go unnoticed or underappreciated due to a lack of self-awareness or external feedback. This oversight can hinder them from honing these skills or leveraging them effectively in their professional endeavours.

The presence of persistent blind spots in individuals can contribute to a state of stagnation. Stagnation occurs when individuals are unable to identify and address areas for improvement or innovation, resulting in a sense of unfulfillment and a lack of progress in their lives. One of the primary ways blind spots contribute to stagnation is by limiting self-awareness. When individuals are unaware of their weaknesses, strengths, and areas for improvement, they may unknowingly resist change or shy away from challenges. The absence of self-awareness may lead to a static existence, where routine replaces growth, and comfort zones remain unchallenged. This stagnant state can foster a sense of monotony and unfulfillment in life. The roots of blind spots often extend from a fundamental lack of self-awareness. This absence of self-awareness, when left unaddressed over time, can impose significant limitations on an individual's capacity to make informed decisions, understand their strengths and weaknesses, and adapt to changing circumstances.

Without a keen understanding of one's own thought patterns, behaviours, and emotional responses, individuals may operate on autopilot, oblivious to the aspects of their personality and actions that may hinder personal and professional growth.

The impact of this diminished self-awareness becomes particularly pronounced when it comes to decision-making. Informed decision-making relies on a clear understanding of personal values, goals, and potential biases. When individuals lack self-awareness, they may make choices without a comprehensive grasp of how these decisions align with their broader aspirations or the potential consequences they might entail. Blind spots obscure this understanding, preventing individuals from leveraging their strengths effectively and addressing areas that require improvement. This lack of insight can impede progress, hinder skill development, and limit an individual's ability to contribute meaningfully to various aspects of life.

The failure to address blind spots can have far-reaching consequences, extending beyond limitations to impact an individual's mental health. Unaddressed blind spots become breeding grounds for stress, anxiety, and an overarching sense of dissatisfaction, creating an ongoing challenge to navigate life without a clear understanding of oneself or the repercussions of one's actions. Stress often arises from the friction between one's perceived reality and the actual outcomes of their decisions and actions. When blind spots obscure a comprehensive understanding of oneself and the factors at play in various situations, individuals may find themselves repeatedly facing unexpected challenges and setbacks. The resulting uncertainty and lack of control contribute to heightened stress levels, creating a persistent state of tension and unease. Anxiety, too, finds fertile ground in unaddressed blind spots. The perpetual unknowns created by a lack of self-awareness can give rise to a constant undercurrent of worry about potential pitfalls, missed opportunities, or interpersonal conflicts. Anxiety may manifest as a nagging feeling that something crucial has been overlooked or as apprehension about the consequences of decisions made in the dark about one's blind spots.

Overall dissatisfaction becomes a pervasive theme when individuals navigate life with unacknowledged blind spots. This dissatisfaction stems from a misalignment between their actions and their underlying values, aspirations, and authentic selves. Without a clear understanding of these fundamental aspects, individuals may find themselves caught in a cycle of unfulfilling pursuits, leading to a pervasive sense of discontentment. The toll on mental health is significant, as the challenges of living with unaddressed blind spots can contribute to emotional exhaustion, a diminished sense of self-worth, and a constant feeling of being overwhelmed. The inability to navigate life with a clear understanding of oneself can exacerbate existing mental health issues or contribute to the development of new ones. Blind spots, those elusive areas of unawareness, can significantly hinder the learning process, acting as barriers that obstruct individuals from recognising gaps in their knowledge or understanding.

One way in which blind spots impede learning is by limiting the capacity to see beyond one's preconceived notions and beliefs. When individuals are unaware of their biases or assumptions, they may approach new information with a closed mindset, unwilling to challenge or expand their existing perspectives. This lack of receptivity obstructs the absorption of diverse ideas and hampers the potential for transformative learning experiences. Furthermore, blind spots can obstruct the development of critical thinking skills. Without a clear understanding of one's cognitive limitations, individuals may struggle to objectively evaluate information, discern fact from opinion, and engage in constructive discourse. This impediment to critical thinking stifles intellectual curiosity and inhibits the depth of understanding that comes from robust, analytical thought processes.

Moreover, blind spots may hinder the cultivation of emotional intelligence, a critical component of both personal and professional growth. Without an understanding of one's emotional reactions or an awareness of others' perspectives, individuals may struggle to navigate complex social dynamics, hindering effective communication and collaboration. The impact of blind spots extends beyond the individual harbouring them, reaching into the dynamics of teams and leadership settings. In such environments, unaddressed blind spots can be particularly detrimental, negatively influencing communication, decision-making, and collaboration.

The long-term impact of blind spots is not confined to the immediate consequences for individuals; it ripples through time, influencing the world we bequeath to those who follow. By recognising these consequences and actively addressing blind spots, we contribute to a more sustainable, equitable, and culturally enriched legacy for the benefit of future generations.

When parents possess blind spots in their communication, it creates a challenging environment for effective interaction with their children. The consequences extend beyond simple miscommunication, often resulting in strained relationships and the potential development of emotional distance. Communication is the foundation of a healthy parent-child relationship, and when hindered by blind spots, several issues may arise. The lack of clear understanding between parents and children can lead to a myriad of problems. Parents may fail to grasp the nuances of their children's thoughts, feelings, and perspectives, resulting in responses that are disconnected and unresponsive to the child's emotional needs. In such situations, unintentional invalidations of the child's experiences may occur. The failure to acknowledge or respect the child's emotions can create a sense of being unheard, fostering an environment where the child's needs are not met, and their emotional well-being is neglected. Moreover, ineffective communication often gives rise to conflicts. Blind spots can contribute to misunderstandings escalating into arguments, further straining the parent-child relationship. The inability to effectively solve problems within the family can leave issues unresolved, perpetuating tension and contributing to an atmosphere of ongoing emotional stress. Trust, a fundamental element of any relationship, can be eroded when communication is lacking. A breakdown in trust occurs when children feel misunderstood or perceive that their concerns are not taken seriously. This breakdown makes it challenging for children to share their thoughts and feelings openly, leading to emotional distance as a protective mechanism. The cumulative effect of persistent misunderstandings and conflicts is the emotional distance between parents and children. This emotional withdrawal can manifest as a coping mechanism for the child, as a means of protecting themselves from the stress and strain of unresolved issues within the family dynamic.

Over time, these challenges in communication can have long-term consequences. Children who experience strained relationships and emotional distance may carry these difficulties into adulthood. The emotional scars from their formative years can impact their own parenting styles and relationships, perpetuating a cycle of communication challenges through generations. Children are perceptive learners, absorbing information about relationships from the dynamics they witness within their families. When parents carry unacknowledged blind spots, these patterns often become unwittingly ingrained in a child's understanding of how relationships function. Dysfunctional relationship dynamics between parents can set a precedent, shaping how children navigate connections with peers, romantic partners, and colleagues later in life.

The influence extends beyond observable behaviours to include communication styles, conflict resolution approaches, and emotional expressions. If parents struggle with these aspects due to unaddressed blind spots, children may adopt similar patterns, inadvertently perpetuating dysfunctional dynamics in their own relationships. Additionally, a parent's level of self-awareness significantly impacts a child's development in this regard. Awareness of personal strengths, weaknesses, and areas for improvement is crucial for fostering a healthy sense of self. Parents who model self-awareness provide a template for their children to follow. Conversely, when parents lack self-awareness due to unacknowledged blind spots, children may find it challenging to develop this essential skill. The absence of a model for self-awareness can hinder a child's ability to navigate personal growth effectively. They may struggle with understanding and managing their own emotions, making it difficult to establish healthy boundaries or communicate effectively in various relationships. This deficiency in self-awareness can have lasting effects, influencing the child's self-esteem, decision-making, and overall emotional well-being into adulthood.

In essence, unacknowledged blind spots in parents not only shape the immediate family dynamics but also leave a lasting imprint on a child's approach to relationships and personal growth. Breaking this cycle requires parents to actively engage in self-reflection, address their own blind spots, and consciously model healthy relationship dynamics and self-awareness for the benefit of their children's future interactions and well-being.

Chapter 17
Creating a Better Future: Nurturing Self-Awareness and Positive Behaviour in Our Children

Creating a better future for our children involves a deliberate focus on nurturing self-awareness and positive behaviour. As parents and caregivers, our role extends beyond providing the basics; it encompasses shaping the emotional intelligence and behavioural foundation upon which our children will build their lives.

Self-awareness plays a pivotal role in the holistic development of individuals, and instilling this quality in our children sets the stage for their lifelong growth and well-being. By creating an environment that actively promotes self-reflection and introspection, we provide our children with valuable tools to navigate the complexities of their emotions, understand their strengths and weaknesses, and form a foundation rooted in personal values. Fostering self-awareness involves encouraging children to explore and articulate their feelings. This could be as simple as engaging in open conversations about their day, asking how certain situations made them feel, and actively listening to their responses. By normalising the expression of emotions, we teach them that it's not only acceptable but crucial to acknowledge and understand what they feel. Similarly, guiding children in identifying their strengths and weaknesses allows them to develop a realistic self-perception. Through constructive feedback and positive reinforcement, we help them build confidence in their abilities while acknowledging areas for improvement. This process contributes to the cultivation of healthy self-esteem, enabling them to approach challenges with resilience and a sense of capability.

Values, the principles that guide our decisions and actions, are integral to self-awareness. Creating a space where children can explore and discuss values helps them understand the importance of integrity, empathy, and other moral principles. This exploration is not about imposing values but rather encouraging thoughtful consideration, allowing children to develop a moral compass that aligns with their authentic selves. One of the most impactful ways to instil self-awareness is through modelling. As parents and caregivers, our commitment to our own self-awareness becomes a potent example for our children. Demonstrating that we, too, are on a continual journey of self-discovery communicates that personal growth is a lifelong pursuit. This modelling underscores the idea that self-awareness is not a destination but a process, emphasising the ongoing value of understanding oneself across various stages of life.

Children are keen observers, and the behaviours they witness in their immediate environment, particularly from their parents and caregivers, leave a lasting impact. The adage "children learn more from what they see than what they are told" underscores the powerful influence of modelled behaviour on a child's development. Modelling positive behaviour, especially in challenging situations, emerges as a potent strategy for instilling values and shaping a child's worldview. The act of modelling positive behaviour involves more than just verbal communication. It is a dynamic process wherein parents and caregivers become living examples of the values they wish to impart. During challenging moments, such as times of stress, conflict, or adversity, the way adults respond becomes a crucial lesson for children. Empathy, an essential aspect of positive behaviour, can be effectively communicated through modelling. When children see their parents empathising with others, understanding different perspectives, and expressing kindness, they internalise these qualities. This helps cultivate a sense of compassion and consideration for others in the child's own actions and interactions. Resilience, the ability to bounce back from setbacks, is another valuable trait that can be instilled through modelling. Demonstrating resilience in the face of challenges teaches children that setbacks are a natural part of life and provides them with a blueprint for navigating difficulties. This modelling helps children develop coping mechanisms and a positive mindset when confronted with obstacles. Effective problem-solving is a skill that children often learn by observing their parents. When adults showcase a constructive approach to addressing issues—whether in personal relationships, work, or daily life—it teaches children the importance of remaining solution-focused. This modelling instils a proactive attitude, encouraging children to view challenges not as insurmountable obstacles but as opportunities for personal and intellectual growth.

The key to successful modelling lies in consistency. When positive behaviour is consistently demonstrated, it becomes an integral part of a child's value system. This modelling goes beyond explicit teaching moments; it becomes a natural and ingrained part of the child's response repertoire.

Open and honest communication serves as the cornerstone of positive relationships, and its significance cannot be overstated in the context of parent-child dynamics. Encouraging our children to express themselves freely, coupled with our commitment to actively listening to their concerns, lays the foundation for a relationship built on trust, understanding, and mutual respect. In fostering an environment where children feel comfortable expressing themselves, we empower them to voice their thoughts, emotions, and experiences. This encouragement goes beyond the superficial; it extends to creating a space where they feel heard and valued. When children believe that their opinions matter, it cultivates a sense of self-worth and reinforces the idea that their perspective is an integral part of the family dynamic. Active listening is a fundamental component of effective communication. By truly engaging with what our children have to say, we convey that their words are not only acknowledged but deeply considered. This active involvement fosters empathy and enhances our understanding of their experiences, allowing us to respond in a more informed and supportive manner.

Modelling effective communication involves more than just the words we use. It encompasses the tone of our voice, body language, and the ability to convey emotions respectfully. By exemplifying how to express thoughts and emotions constructively, we teach our children the art of communication as a tool for connection rather than conflict.

Moreover, our commitment to expressing our own thoughts and emotions respectfully becomes a powerful lesson. Children learn not only from what is said but also from how it is said. Demonstrating a calm and respectful approach, especially in moments of disagreement or conflict, reinforces the idea that differences can be addressed without compromising the fundamental respect we have for one another. This modelled behaviour has a lasting impact on our children's interpersonal connections beyond the family unit. As they venture into friendships, romantic relationships, and professional environments, the communication skills they have observed at home become a guiding influence. The ability to express themselves clearly, listen attentively, and navigate disagreements respectfully contributes to their overall success in building positive relationships outside the family.

Empathy, as a fundamental skill, plays a pivotal role in shaping positive behaviour, particularly in the context of child development. It goes beyond understanding one's own emotions; it involves recognising and sharing the feelings of others. Instilling empathy in children not only fosters a sense of compassion but also lays the groundwork for cooperative and considerate behaviour. Helping children understand and share the feelings of others is a multi-faceted process. It begins with creating an awareness of emotions, both their own and those of people around them. Through open discussions and age-appropriate conversations, children can learn to recognise various emotions, understand their nuances, and appreciate the diversity of feelings that individuals experience. Instilling compassion and cooperation is a natural outcome of developing empathy. When children grasp that others may feel joy, sadness, or frustration just like they do, it builds a foundation for compassion. This understanding prompts them to consider the emotional well-being of others, fostering a sense of interconnectedness and shared humanity. Encouraging acts of kindness becomes a practical application of empathy. Simple gestures, such as helping a friend in need, sharing toys, or expressing concern for someone upset, reinforce the empathetic connection. These actions not only demonstrate care for others but also create a positive environment where kindness is valued and reciprocated.

Emphasising the impact of their actions on others is crucial in cultivating a sense of social responsibility. By connecting empathetic understanding to the consequences of their behaviour, children learn that their actions have the power to influence the well-being of those around them. This awareness encourages responsible decision-making and reinforces the idea that positive behaviour contributes to a harmonious and supportive community. Moreover, empathy extends beyond direct interactions to include an appreciation for diversity and an understanding of different perspectives. Teaching children to empathise with individuals from various backgrounds, cultures, and experiences broadens their worldview. It promotes tolerance, reduces prejudice, and encourages inclusivity, fostering a socially responsible mindset.

The establishment of clear and reasonable boundaries is a fundamental component of fostering positive behaviour in children. These boundaries serve as guidelines that not only teach children about respect for themselves and others but also provide a framework for responsible decision-making. The consistency in enforcing these boundaries plays a crucial role in creating a sense of security and predictability for children as they navigate their world. Teaching children about respect begins with helping them understand the importance of valuing themselves and those around them. Clear boundaries communicate expectations for behaviour, both in terms of how children should treat themselves and how they should interact with others. This includes considerations for personal space, communication, and recognising and appreciating diversity. Additionally, boundaries introduce the concept of consequences, linking actions to outcomes. By establishing a cause-and-effect relationship, children learn that their decisions have repercussions. Teaching them about the potential impact of their actions on themselves and others encourages thoughtful consideration before making choices. This understanding forms the basis for responsible decision-making as children learn to weigh the potential consequences of their behaviour.

Consistency in enforcing boundaries is essential for several reasons. Firstly, it provides children with a reliable and predictable environment. Knowing what is expected of them creates a sense of security, helping them feel more in control of their surroundings. This predictability contributes to a stable emotional foundation, fostering a positive and supportive atmosphere. Consistent enforcement of boundaries also reinforces the importance of rules and expectations. When children observe that rules are consistently applied, they are more likely to internalise the values behind those rules. This internalisation sets the stage for the development of intrinsic motivation, where children understand and choose positive behaviour because they recognise its inherent value, not just to avoid consequences.

Encouraging children to take on age-appropriate responsibilities is a powerful strategy for nurturing a sense of independence and self-efficacy. By assigning tasks that align with their abilities, we provide them with opportunities to develop essential life skills and cultivate a can-do attitude. This empowerment not only enables them to tackle challenges effectively but also fosters resilience and a positive mindset that will serve them well in various aspects of their lives. When children are entrusted with responsibilities, it signals to them that their contributions matter and that they can contribute meaningfully to the functioning of the family or community. This sense of purpose fosters budding independence, allowing them to see themselves as capable individuals with the capacity to take on and complete tasks.

In addition to building confidence, allowing children to shoulder responsibilities nurtures resilience. They learn that encountering difficulties or setbacks is a natural part of taking on tasks, and these challenges provide growth opportunities. Overcoming obstacles contributes to the development of resilience, teaching children that setbacks are not insurmountable barriers but rather stepping stones to greater competence and self-assurance. Fostering a can-do attitude goes beyond specific tasks; it influences how children approach challenges in various aspects of their lives. This attitude becomes a mindset—a lens through which they perceive difficulties not as insurmountable problems but as opportunities to learn, grow, and build their capabilities.

Promoting a growth mindset in children is a transformative approach that goes beyond academic achievement—it cultivates a love for learning and resilience in the face of setbacks. By emphasising that abilities can be developed through dedication and hard work, we instil in them a profound belief in the power of effort. This mindset not only shapes their academic pursuits but also fosters a positive and adaptive approach to challenges across various facets of life. A growth mindset is rooted in the understanding that intelligence and abilities are not fixed traits but can be cultivated through learning and effort. Encouraging children to see challenges as opportunities for growth rather than insurmountable obstacles creates a mindset that thrives on curiosity and a passion for acquiring new knowledge.

This approach instils a love for learning—a genuine enthusiasm for exploring new concepts, tackling unfamiliar subjects, and embracing the joy of intellectual discovery. When children are encouraged to view learning as an ongoing journey rather than a destination, they become more resilient and open-minded, valuing the process of acquiring skills and knowledge as much as the outcomes.

The idea that intelligence is not fixed but malleable encourages children to persevere in the face of setbacks. Instead of viewing mistakes as failures, they learn to see them as stepping stones toward improvement. This resilience not only enhances their ability to bounce back from setbacks but also fosters a positive attitude toward challenges, promoting a mindset that embraces the process of learning and growing. Promoting a growth mindset is about more than just academic achievement; it shapes the way children perceive themselves and the world. It influences their self-esteem, self-efficacy, and overall outlook on life. By cultivating a belief in their capacity to develop skills through dedication, we empower them with a mindset that not only propels academic success but also lays the foundation for a positive and adaptive approach to the challenges they encounter in the dynamic journey of life.

As parents, we might not have had the right role models or guidance, but we have the power to change the course of the future. By reclaiming our influence and actively instilling self-awareness, positive behaviour, effective communication, empathy, and personal responsibility in our children, we can create a ripple effect that shapes the legacy of the next generation. Let's seize this opportunity to be the architects of a future where our children construct lives that are not only fulfilling and meaningful but also reflective of the positive changes we have introduced.

About the Author

Farzaneh Ghadirian, an Australian immigrant for over two decades, brings a unique perspective to her writing. With a childhood passion for books, she authored her very first book at the tender age of eight, setting up a makeshift library in her parents' storeroom. Little did she anticipate that writing would become a significant part of her life.

After years of personal growth and self-realisation, Farzaneh rediscovered her love for writing. Her journey took a spiritual turn, as she embarked on a path of self-discovery, breaking away from a low-frequency existence that offered predictability but hindered personal growth. Escaping her previous programming, she sought her true inner self, leading to a profound transformation.

Farzaneh has authored a diverse range of books, including a memoir, a philosophy book delving into the interconnection of mind and body with mesmerising life wisdom quotations and captivating photos, along with three children's books. All of her works are available on platforms such as Amazon. In her latest creation, *Intergenerational Blind Spots: Bridging the Gap for a Unified Tomorrow*, she seamlessly integrates her perspectives as both an author and a certified life coach.

In this enlightening exploration, Farzaneh delves into the intricate dynamics shaping our shared experiences across generations. With a focus on psychology, behaviour transmission, and the consequences of our actions, she uncovers often-overlooked blind spots influencing our understanding of one another. Through personal narratives, research, and anecdotes, Farzaneh provides a roadmap for overcoming the challenges arising when diverse perspectives converge.

Intergenerational Blind Spots is not just an examination of the impacts of blind spots but a beacon of hope, fostering connection and unity. Farzaneh encourages readers to recognise the strengths of each generation, building bridges across divides for a harmonious future that integrates the wisdom of the past with the promises of tomorrow.

www.ingramcontent.com/pod-product-compliance
Lightning Source LLC
Chambersburg PA
CBHW051436290426
44109CB00016B/1585